The Scattered Italians

REFLECTIONS ON A HEROIC JOURNEY

by
Thomas Gambino

authorHOUSE

AuthorHouse™
1663 Liberty Drive
Bloomington, IN 47403
www.authorhouse.com
Phone: 1 (800) 839-8640

Published by AuthorHouse 10/27/2017

ISBN: 978-1-4259-6964-6 (sc)

Print information available on the last page.

This book is printed on acid-free paper.

I have written this book to honor my family,
and all Italians
who have been scattered throughout the world.

Acknowledgements

The following titles were invaluable in assisting me to better understand and recount this significant and compelling story. However, not all of the reference material examined has been noted.

Gambino, Richard, Blood of My Blood, Double Day & Company, 1974

Barzini, Luigi, The Italians, Atheneum, 1965

Willensky, Elliot, When Brooklyn Was the World, Harmony Books, 1986

Ciongoli, Kenneth, A & Parini, Jay, Passage to Liberty, Regan Books, 2002

Moramarco, Federico & Stephen, Italian Pride, Kensington Publishing Corp, 2000

Fiorini, Flavio, Storia Illustrata Del Fascismo, Giunti Editore, 2000

Correnti, Santi, Palermo D'Allora, Longanesi Editore, 1979

Caesar, Gaius, Julius, De Bellum Gallicum , 58-51 BC

Virgil, The Aeneid, 19BC

Gibbon, Eduard, The Decline and Fall of The Roman Empire, 1776

Aleghieri, Dante, The Divine Comedy, 1308

Peet, John, Addio Dolce Vita, The Economist, November 2005 edition.

A note of special thanks goes out to my wife Catherine and son Nicola for their patience and support, and to my good friend Armand Pelletier for his editorial assistance.

Prologue

Our literary voyage, which takes place over three millennia, is aimed at arriving at conclusions that will go far in explaining who we are as scattered Italians, and why we act out life's drama as we do. We will be in the company of some of the titans of history, along with the beloved people of the Gambino and Sparacino families, to whom I belong. We shall experience firsthand how we overcame fate's erratic and perverse inconsistencies, which culminated in an extraordinary cultural and historical upheaval; the forced migration of the Italian people.

During the latter period of the 1800s through to the early 1900s, Italy was set upon by enormous catastrophes that were the result of mankind's folly. The outcome affected an entire nation, as well as the world at large, causing a Diaspora, or a scattering abroad of the Italian people and their descendants. Few were fortunate enough to return to reclaim the resulting lost identity and citizenship. Our story touches all of us, for we all seek, at one time or another, our true persona during life's journey.

We in the West are the recipients of a common civilization, much of it bequeathed to us by Italy. Think of it; many of the laws we live by, much of the music, art, poetry and food we enjoy, myriad scientific achievements, and many of the languages we speak originated from this divine peninsula surrounded by the azure Mediterranean Sea. The Roman Empire, as well as the consequences of the Renaissance, continues to define our common inheritance and influence our daily lives. Consider that a large percentage of the English language, the present *lingua franca*, originated from Latin, our great mother tongue.* Our people discovered the Americas!

Dante Alighieri, Francesco Petrarca, Giovanni Boccaccio, Niccolo Machiavelli, Leonardo da Vinci, Michelangelo Buonarroti, Fra Angelico, Giuseppe Verdi, Gioacchino Rossini, Antonio Vivaldi, Arturo Toscanini, Galileo Galilei, Alessandro Volta, Gugliermo Marconi, Enrico Fermi, Marco Polo, Cristofero Colombo, and Amerigo Vespucci were but a few of the great Italian personalities of literature, art, music, science and discovery. It is my firm belief that without Italy and the Italians, the world would surely have remained dark, cold, unknown, and uncivilized.

I am truly challenged by the task of recounting this tale objectively, as I am Italian, and therefore I confess that I am particularly subject to Italy's many charms.

Your author-Q.D.V.B.
Kailua, Hawaii

---

* Examples of Latin can be found in the glossary.

Contents

Allegorical Sculpture Vittorio Emanuelle II Bridge Rome

The Beginning

Our journey, whose history unfolds over three millennia, requires that we have an understanding of some of its highlights. Hence, we shall uncover some of the reasons why things might have happened as they did, or, for that matter, why they happened at all.

Where does one begin when confronted with such a massively rich culture and history occurring over such an enormously long time? What were the Italian people like in times past; when did their history start to take hold; and where and how? Who were the major players of their drama?

Many *cognoscenti* would view 754 BC as the real beginning of the Italians. After all, Romulus killed his brother Remus and founded Rome in that year, so the legend goes. But mighty Rome was not the beginning of our people, for there were many developed cultures and societies thriving in the divine peninsula starting well before 2000 BC. The Sicels, Umbrians, Samites, and Etruscans, to name but a few, were well on their way to establishing control over diverse parts of Italy. They were masters of ceramics and metal-making, and had advanced strategies in waging wars; they were traders with merchants of other lands. They spoke mysterious non-Latin languages. They had rules, mores, customs, and religions dissimilar from the creeds and culture that developed during and after the Roman period.

From approximately 2000 BC to about 89 BC, these non-Roman cultures and societies held sway over parts of Italy independently. With the advent of Roman expansionism, however, numerous different groups united in opposing militarily the Roman Imperial Mandate. Their union may be considered an Italic League of sorts. Hence, here we find the very origin of Italy. The League was, at first, able to successfully combat Rome's vaunted legions. For they knew how to fight in a guerilla, hit-and-run fashion, which confused the orderly battle plans of the masterful Romans. Who would have guessed at that point that Rome would be triumphant? The great Roman General Lucius Cornelius Sulla (138 BC-78 BC), however, was very resourceful in tailoring his battle plans to confront the valiant warriors of the League, and defeated them completely on the Via Antica near Mirabella Eclano in approximately 89 BC. That put an end to any independent aspirations on the League's part. Much of the peninsula was now dominated by Rome for all practical purposes.

The brilliance of the Roman triumph, however, lay with their willingness to reach out to the vanquished warriors who survived, leaving them to run their own internal affairs while at the same time receiving their allegiances. Eventually they were made to enjoy full Roman citizenship, with all its inherent advantages. It was a complete cultural, societal, and military conquest by the Romans, which served as an example for conquering the entire known world and giving birth to the idea of a common *patria*-one coin, one tongue, and one people.

SPQR-*Senatus Populus Quiritium Romanus* (*The* Senate and the People of Rome)

With the fall of the Italic League, we now are confronted with the glory that was Rome. The Latin tribe of the famous seven hills, in one way or another, influenced the destiny of the world for over two thousand years, and continues to this day. At one point in time, over one-fourth of the world population was ruled by the omniscient Caesars. It is not my intent to review the entire period, which has been amply recorded elsewhere. However, since Italy became Roman and we trace our lineage from Italy, I feel it appropriate to review some of the more salient parts of Rome's history and to examine how it affected us all.

Let us first appreciate some of that history, which produced so many titans for the world's stage. If one were to read Virgil's crowning epic story, *The Aeneid* (19 BC), then in a sense we must thank Helen of Troy for the founding of Rome. As the myth expounds, Aeneas, Prince of Troy, escaped the fall of his city to the Greeks who waged war against it for abducting Helen. Upon arrival in Latium he and his companions married Latin women which in turn gave rise to the mighty Roman race. Hence, Rome and the world were forever influenced and indebted to a young woman's great beauty. How very appropriate, as the city is excitingly pleasing to the eye.

Rome then became the mother of our civilization by having sons of exceptional abilities nourished by her mild climate and other well-defined attributes. How then could we expect the other ancient Northern European cultures and societies of that time to evolve to such heights of sophistication when the people of that vast area were struggling to survive their horrendous climatic conditions? The dark gray skies and cold wet air were not mere inconveniences, but real challenges to their very lives. It then is not hard to comprehend the contrast between the ancient Northern Europeans, who were painted savages living in crude huts, caves and forests, from the peoples of Rome who were living, in some cases, in white marble castles with time and the luxury to evolve a superior existence in all things.

Some of Rome's Famous Sons of the Past

To better understand the true greatness of early Rome, we need to look at some of her famous sons of the past, those very people that shaped our civilization by their actions and deeds. How difficult is this task in choosing whom to visit? There were innumerable emperors, consuls, and generals of the first order. By being astute we can perhaps focus on those who changed our future world completely and forever.

There was, in North Africa, a small patch of desert named Zama, which was merely 50 miles from Tunis, Tunisia's present capital. Here, in the year 202 BC, two world cultures clashed. The mighty armies of Carthage, lead by the fearsome general Hannibal Barca (247-182 BC), faced the smaller but more nimble Roman Legions of General Cornelius Scipio (236-184 BC). This battle would conclude the Second Punic War and lay open the rest of the known world to conquest for the winner of this contest. Carthage, founded by the ancient Phoenicians, who were of Semite ancestry, was situated on the North African Coast just south of Italy, and had many of the advantageous climatic conditions, as did Rome. It also had a proud history and developed culture going back many centuries. She was a true contender, if there ever was one, to defeat Rome. The Senate of Rome (Rome was in these days a republic) sent Scipio to Africa with a mandate to conquer Carthage once and for all.

The sun rose in the eastern sky as Hannibal charged the Roman line with eighty war elephants. The Romans, at first, were stunned, but then recovered and maneuvered the beasts into human alleyways and confused them by making loud noises. The battle raged all day and was not decided until the Roman cavalry attacked to the rear of the Carthaginians. By nightfall the Roman Eagle was triumphant…Scipio would be called, in honor of his victory, Scipio Africanus, and the world would be conquered by Rome. Hence, the culture and character of the to-be-conquered world would become Roman, not Carthaginian.

No story of Rome could be imagined without discussing the imposing personality of Gaius Julius Caesar (100-44 BC). Caesar was considered divine by his soldiers, a god. He was also dictator, high priest, and consul. Europe, Asia, and Africa were among his many conquests. It is said that at the time of his assassination he was about to conquer the Parthian Kingdom (present day Iran) and possibly go on to India, as did Alexander the Great. Brave Caesar was at once brilliant, resolute, and, above all, a supreme leader of men. His soldiers would enter into battle shouting, "Caesar leads; we fear nothing," for they felt that his godly presence would bring good fortune and victory to them and Rome, as well.

Yes, Caesar had a superior understanding of military maneuver, but so did others; what made him stand as commander above all those others? Simply, he was a good performer! Truth is what you believe it to be, and he, along with his cohorts, believed that he was divine and acted the part.

His outstanding personal courage was passed on to his men, making them bigger then life. If you fight for your god, you become in a sense an extension of the deity. You yourself become superhuman or god-like. There was a living presence that was direct, personal, and profound. It made men take great risks, endure any hardship, and face death with enormous courage. What barbarian could possibly overcome these men who fought like gods? Caesar's legions were greatly outnumbered in most of their military engagements with the Barbarian hoard, but never succumbed to mere numbers. They feared nothing, for they had Caesar leading them on to victory.

An example of Caesar's *modus operandi* follows; I have borrowed from Caesar's own writings, Book VII of *De Bellum Gallicum* (*The Commentaries of the Gallic Wars, 58-51 BC*).

There had to be a fundamental strategy that Caesar employed in overcoming the huge number of barbarians arrayed against him and his men. It is true that the tribes of Gaul, which once inhabited what is now modern-day France, were not sophisticated in warfare and were untrustworthy to their own kind. They often would simply charge the Roman line and be slaughtered by Caesar's disciplined and well-trained troops. Yet the numerical differential of, at times, six to one could have been deadly to the Roman cause if pursued wisely. Hence, Caesar used the "divide and conquer" rule to overcome the Barbarian's mathematical advantage. Historically, the forty-three tribes of Gaul oftentimes fought among themselves, and hence, by siding with one over the other, Caesar reduced the numerical edge of his many enemies. Some tribes became romanized, with their leaders speaking

Latin. In time, their very offspring would become the greatest defenders of Rome, for they became Roman citizens and defended what became the Roman Empire. Once again, we have total societal and cultural conquest by Rome by their application of enlightened rule.

But we are getting ahead of ourselves. A young and able barbarian king called Vencingetorex (75BC-46BC) of the Arvian tribe challenged the good fortunes of the Romans. He convinced many other tribes to form a common front against Caesar and anoint him leader. He reasoned that over a quarter of a million barbarian warriors, if united, could easily defeat a mere forty thousand Romans. The crucial battle took place near a town called Alesia in central Gaul near modern day Dijon, France, in September of 52 BC. Skirmishes took place most of the day until Vencingetorex decided to retire inside Alesia, which was a town situated on top of a high hill and protected by walls. He thought that he would be able to run raids with his eighty thousand troops into the Roman line while waiting for the rest of his quarter-million men to arrive and strike the Romans from the rear. Caesar had other ideas, however, and built a double wall, called a circumvallation, which was eleven miles in length which blockaded and encircled the hilltop barbarians while also protecting his rear from enemy reinforcements. The day arrived with a sea of barbarians striking at Caesar's positions. The Roman walls at first held, until a weak point was found and attacked simultaneously by almost all of the Barbarians. Caesar, in great haste, sent in his reserve of three thousand to fill the breach. Alas, it was too much for the valiant Roman soldiers and they began to waiver. This could have resulted in total and ruinous defeat for the Romans. However, Caesar, with great courage, mounted his steed, and, wearing a scarlet cape to identify him, charged pell-mell into the Barbarians. His men, seeing this act of heroism, regained their composure, followed their leader, and won the day for him. Vencingetorex was defeated, sent his sword to Caesar, and knelt at his feet in utter defeat. The world had changed completely and forever because of Caesar's actions. Gaul did not remain barbaric but instead became Roman and civilized.

Great Caesar, in the end, would be betrayed and assassinated by his own people, the corrupt power-hungry Senate, in Rome. When I lived in Rome (1975-1983), I would think to myself, as I mourned Caesar's assassination every Ides of March, "Why am I alone in doing this?" There, at the Ara di Caesar (the altar where Caesar's body was cremated), dressed somberly, with book in hand, reading of the dastardly act of betrayal, I felt real sorrow, not so much for the historic act of betrayal over which I had no control, but because there were no other Romans there to honor his spirit.

Caesar! Caesar! Great shield of Rome, Sword of Conquest,
the evil deed shall live in infamy
and be remembered by those who love you!--your author

Emperor Constantine The Great (272-337AD) was another audacious world game changer. After the Apostles he was arguably the most historically significant mortal responsible for the growth and success of Christianity. Until his appearance on the world stage Christianity was considered an exotic eastern sect. It was illegal and poorly received by the masses making up the Empire. What did Emperor Constantine do to change that perception and why?

Lets review the salient issues which resulted in the more then 2.2 billion Christians worshipping around the world today. There is a bridge, Ponte Milvio, in the northern area of Rome, which strides the Tiber River. Here an epic battle took place (312AD) between Constantine and his rival for power, Maxentius. Legend has it that Constantine saw in the heavens a cross with the script "In Hoc Signo Vinces" (In this sign you shall conquer) Maxentius retreated before the conquering Constantine and was killed escaping. In deed, the sign of the cross assured victory. By the Edict of Milan (313AD) Constantine bestowed upon Christianity the status of State religion. Paganism was finished, the language of the Church of Rome was now Latin, the lingua franca of the known world. The formally eastern sect flourished due to Roman excellent roads, communication, formal structure and legitimacy. Was it God's plan?

The exceptional sons of Rome are many, and we have briefly visited three of my favorite. There were many, many others... Hadrian, Aralias and Agrippa, to name but a few. Their stories require volumes to explore, but we do not have that luxury, nor is it our goal. It is enough to know that their empire, consisting of both eastern and western spheres, lasted nearly two thousand years. It could be argued that the Empire morphed into other forms after the fall in the west (476 AD). For instance, the Holy Roman Empire (800-1806), which came afterwards, was neither holy, nor Roman; however, it followed in the tradition of the original. The Vatican is yet another example of the Empire's longevity in its modern form. The Pope is called Pontefex Maximus; the Church speaks Latin and is universal. Perhaps, in the end, the Roman Empire was created for a higher purpose. Was it God's will? It is whispered to this very day among Romans:

> "When the Coliseum falls, so shall Rome.
> When Rome falls, so shall the World!"

A Look at Rome Today

Rome is located in a physically beautiful setting, situated on its seven hills. It enjoys a mild climate, allowing for an uplifting feel to everyday living. The light is very special, being bright, clear, and stimulating. It makes one feel younger, more vital, and more in contact with life itself. One has a sense of well-being, leading to a feeling of happiness and a joy of life. There is a spell produced that appeals to the human spirit and enhances everything you do. This rapture and delight can bring forth the best we as humans have to offer. This grand geography and clement weather then gives rise to an innate psychology and distinguished character that is far superior to many others.

There is, then, this exceptional quality permeating Rome that is presented daily to the first-time visitor, as well as to the locals. Experiencing the Eternal City in the early morning hours, with its ever-changing hues of pink and rose colors splashed on endless numbers of cupolas, towers, arches, and fountains, calls to the senses. As the Roman sun rises, the human spirit absorbs its warmth. It is like a mother's embrace, affectionate and lasting. I often marveled at the sense of completeness I felt as I walked from my apartment, located within the walls of the fourteenth-century Torlonia Palace. There was the inevitable near miss with an on-rushing Vespa scooter as I made my way to Café Settimiana, which is partially built within the ancient Savian walls. These over-two-thousand-year-old walls protected Rome during Barbarian attacks. How accommodating Ferruccio, the cashier, was as I strode through the café door he would cry out an order to his colleague, *"caffe` per il dottore".* Once at the counter, I was greeted again by the honorific title of *"Dottore"* (doctor) and served with great ceremony an excellent espresso. Dressed in my latest Zegna suit and holding a Gucci attaché case in hand, I would reflect on how special my life had become. I was bewitched early on by the charm and beauty of my adopted country and city. Although many years have passed since I gave up residence in Rome, when I revisit and go for my espresso at my usual café, the ritual is replayed for me as if I had never left the local scene. Ferruccio never questioned my extended absences, as he could never contemplate that I could leave Rome permanently and assumed that I merely moved to another part of the city.

After a brief walk through cabled stoned alleyways, I would arrive at Piazza Sonino and Bus 56, which would transport me across the famous Tiber River, past Renaissance palaces, Baroque buildings, and numerous fountains. Arriving finally at my stop at Piazza Barbarini, a cacophony of sounds would meet me as the sidewalks were filled with Romans rushing off to work while engrossed in their locally-accented conversation, oftentimes gesticulating wildly. Shop owners were busy opening up their metal grates, exposing small shops of all sorts. The food markets would be in full swing, with locals selecting the fresh condiments for their repast for that evening, arguing all the time that the price was too high or the produce not fit for their pallet. I would, oftentimes, stand in the mist of the swirl that was taking place in the market, just to absorb the energy and be part of the scene. This practice often resulted in my buying some greens for a dinner that I would never cook and most probably gave to my doorman. I was embarrassed to admit that I was just there because I enjoyed playing the role and being part of the show so very much.

Your author with Gaius Julius Caesar, Rome, 1975

All Roads Lead to Rome

The overwhelming achievement of the Romans was their development of Western civilization. The *Pax Romana* (Roman Peace) allowed for the elevation of the human spirit. Refinement, love of letters, science, commerce, principles of life and how to live and behave, and the ability to travel and conduct commerce in a lawful manner were spread throughout the Empire and are still with us today. Peoples of different lands and cultures shared unknown flowers, fruits, and animal types. The very grapes and knowledge that produce famous French wines came from the Romans over two thousand years ago. The Mediterranean Sea, known then as *Mare Nostrum* (Our Sea), became a safe conduit of products and ideas. It took only seven days to sail from Egypt to Rome and, likewise, from the straights of Gibraltar. All major roads lead to Rome, with some still in use to this very day. Via Appia, Via Tiburtina, and Via Aurelio are but a few of the famous roads, which carried the lifeblood of the Roman Empire. The same tongue was spoken on the shores of the river Tiber as on the shores of the river Thames; the same poetry was read and rhetoric heard. A single coin was used, and a common set of laws governed all. The Romans additionally adopted the Greek school of philosophy, ensuring that it would be handed down to us today and future generations. Much of the Western World, as we know it, is Rome's legacy to us.

Christian Rome

The Roman Catholic Church is centered in Vatican City, which is surrounded by the glorious city of Rome. Although an independent state, it occupies only approximately 109 acres in area with close to nine hundred citizens, including the Pope. Its most striking feature is the Basilica, the largest such structure in the world, created by the architect Bramante in 1506 and capped by the dome, or *copula*, designed by Michelangelo. The enormous Piazza, which can accommodate two hundred fifty thousand people, is framed by Bernini's Doric-pillared colonnade, which reaches out to welcome all of humanity. The impact on the first-time visitor, Christian or non-Christian, is overwhelming, as it is meant to be.

Christian Rome, for over two thousand years, has been a beacon of light in a cold, dark, and unfriendly world, and continues to guide over one billion of the faithful while influencing the rest of humanity. One had only to witness the funeral of His Holiness Pope John Paul II (1920-2005), to realize what an extraordinary hold the Pontifex Maximus and thus, Rome has on all of us. Over four million souls went to Rome to pay their respects and over two billion watched on television. Rome played its role once again as the center of influence over the entire world. Although much has changed over the thousands of years, Rome still rules.

There is no question that the Pope's ecclesial authority is supreme. There is simply no other entity that can compete with his impact. There was a time, however, when popes behaved more like Caesar than popes. After the fall of the Western Empire in 476 AD, Italy was in chaos, with the Barbarian tribes plundering the land and destroying all civilized forms of life they came into contact with. The Romans turned to their pope for protection and order. Hence, for many centuries to come, the popes' emphasis was more on armies, alliances, and statecraft, besides the usual ecclesial concerns. To be sure, there were scoundrels along with saints that served, and included men from politically powerful and rich families, as well. For instance, Pope Alexander VI (1431-1503), of the Borgia family, was a swinger enjoying the company of the ladies, drink, treasure, and the arts. He had many illegitimate children, which, through his intervention, became powerful leaders in their own right. He spent vast sums on the grace and beauty of the Vatican. He was responsible for commissioning Pinturicchio in decorating the outstanding Borgia Apartments.

It was Pope Julius II (1443-1513), truly a soldier at heart, who started the rebuilding of the Basilica in 1506. It took 120 years to complete, honoring him as a true patron of the arts. His nickname was Julius the Terrible. My favorite of these Renaissance popes was a Medici prince called Pope Leo X (1475-1521). He was constantly fighting to keep Italy free of foreign control. He spent, without limit, on wars and the refurbishing of the Vatican, as well. Pope Leo X often enjoyed elaborate dinners and supposedly said, "God gave us the Papacy; let us enjoy it!" In order to raise money for this exuberant rule, Pope Leo X sold indulgences, which are pardons for sins both present and future. Imagine what kind of action ensued with that kind of insurance policy.

The first crusade occurred during the period of 1095-1100. It was proclaimed by Pope Urban II (1042-1099), in order to take by force Jerusalem and the surrounding areas. It was all-out war of the Western European countries and their peoples against the Muslims. It was successful, as Jerusalem was conquered in 1099. Pope Urban II exclaimed, "It is God's will!" Again, we can visualize the morphing of a pope into a Caesar, commanding an army and conquering lands for the Empire-- this time, supposedly, for religious purposes. The Roman Emperor Titus (40 AD-81 AD), a pagan conqueror of Jerusalem countless centuries before and the originator of Diaspora, could not have been more pleased.

By the 17th century, the temporal powers of the popes began to decline as nationalism took hold all over Europe. Henceforth, the European leaders representing states would not accept directives from the Vatican without question. Once again, change was in the air, culminating in the Lateran treaties signed in 1929 between Pope Pius XI (1857-1939) and the Italian Government of Benito Mussolini (1883-1945). All temporal powers were gone, leaving only the ecclesial. Was it God's will?

My Personal Road to Rome

Perhaps in my case it was God's will, for in 1975 I was presented with an opportunity to live in the city of the popes. While in New York City and employed by Alitalia Airlines, I became aware of an employment opportunity in Rome with United Airlines. I could not wait a moment and decided to act and gamble it all by asking our personnel manager, Joe McGhee, to immediately inquire. He did and was told the job was tentatively filled. Luck was, however, with me, as United Airlines was willing to do one more in-terview. I was wild with anticipation.

As destiny would have it, I was going on a business trip to Rome; hence, a side trip to London, the site of the interview, was easily arranged. The night before my trip to London and the interview was filled with great anxiety and sleeplessness. I found myself walking aimlessly through the empty Roman city streets in the early morning hours. What would I say? How would I approach the challenge I was so sure I could not overcome successfully the following day?

After wondering and thinking, I found myself in the middle of St. Peter's Square quite alone, as it was approxi-mately two o'clock in the morning. The square, as previously mentioned, can hold up to two hundred fifty thousand people and I was the only one there. Rather than feel alone, I felt a sense of welcome and a presence of some sort. Nor-mally indifferent religiously, I fell to my knees and prayed for the strength and wisdom I so very much needed. To this day, I remember the exact spot. The stars, moon, and soft lighting splashing against the buildings and statues of saints was comforting. After some twenty minutes of prayer and thanks, I rose and felt a kind of fullness about me. I was ready for anything, for I felt imbued with an inner force.

London is a dreary city, in my opinion, with its terrible weather, poor cuisine, and what passes for English humor. I never liked the place or, with few exceptions, the people, but I would have traveled to Timbuktu for this occasion. As expected, the top executive of United in Europe, Dave Robertson, administered the interview. The questions and answers were rather mundane until Dave asked me for the reason I wanted to leave Alitalia Airlines to join United Airlines. My reply was immediate and filled with conviction: "I do not want to leave my company; you have to convince me to join yours." I got the job! I was on my own personal road to Rome. My life had changed forever. There was an invisible hand at work and things would never be the same for me again.

Many months later, while talking with Dave privately, he reminded me of our interview and my crisp answer to his question. He also mentioned that he had posed that question to other airline executives who had also applied for the job. Apparently, they were not as filled with conviction as I was, and in some cases spoke poorly of their company. This, he told me, convinced him of my integrity. I never told him that my answer was the result, in part, of my Italophile tendencies and a true belief that we at Alitalia were superior to most. To this day, I feel the same way and probably would answer in the same fashion. This firm adherence to an unwritten code of behavior developed a sense of integrity, which, once acquired, would never abandon me no matter what I was to face in the future. This, in my opinion, was due to the reacquiring of my inherited culture and exposure to Italian society in general.

Darkness and Light

The Dark Ages

The fall of the Roman Empire in the West (476 AD) was a major catastrophe for mankind. For all practical purposes, civilized society ceased to exist. The Northern hordes burned, pillaged, and destroyed all that was before them. Whole cities were ransacked and mutilated by these beastly invaders. The human spirit was engulfed in an epoch of calamity that would change the known world of enlightenment to the brutish and dreadful world of the Barbarian. The dark ages of feudalism was born. The resulting new kings and the petty nobility were all dependent on the serfs to support their privileged lifestyle. The human condition descended to its lowest nadir. There was little commerce, few exchanges of ideas, no mother tongue, no single coin or laws. There was, instead, great suffering, poverty, and plague for most of the people of the former proud Empire.

This was the time when Latin was no longer taught, for there were no schools for the masses. Hence, local dialects were born, which eventually resulted in the major Romance tongues spoken today. Just think, Italian, French, Spanish, Portuguese, and Romanian grew from Latin as vulgar tongues, or *patois*, into new languages spoken by millions.

The Dark Ages and its horrendous setting would last from 479 AD to approximately 1000 AD, and is replete with many tales of woe and misadventures. Fortunately, it is not the period that interests us in this text, and, therefore, with the reader's indulgence, I will delve into the next period of Italian graciousness and charm.

The Renaissance

The catastrophic Dark Ages were followed by the Renaissance (1300-1700). It was perhaps the richest development of human individuality known to man, and was centered in the Italian city of Florence. The thirteenth to the seventeenth centuries were witness to this incredible rebirth of culture and civilization that enlightened Europe once again.

The time of the wild barbarian hordes had ended centuries before. Many tribes returned north across the Alps once their chief had died. Those who stayed behind were absorbed into the local populations. To this day, traces of their genetic pool can be seen. It is no wonder that the tall, blond, blue-eyed Italian is generally found in the north of the peninsula, while the dark, bronzed Mediterranean type is found in the south. My mother, when presenting my blue-eyed father to my Sicilian grandfather, was greeted with "This is the one you pick-- this one with blue eyes?" It loses a lot in the translation, but indicates to what extent the invaders impacted the locals many centuries after the fact.

Italy in the thirteenth century comprised a series of independent city-states, and regions, as well as the Papal States ruled by the Vatican. Some were despotic, while others were democratic. The great sea-faring republics of Genoa and Venice come to mind. They were competitive, often trying to upend the other. Commerce flourished, creating an environment of humanistic revival. The cities brought forth renewal and excitement. Brilliance in the arts, letters, science, music, and architecture were due in part to the freed spirit of a vigorous and talented populace. Social betterment and progress of the individual added to this enduring value of the human spirit. The prince was often at the center of this revival, spending lavishly on glorious works of art. We need to mention but only a few of the great artists of this period. Da Vinci, Donatello, Botticelli, Michelangelo, and Raphael top the list of many hundreds of individuals who attest to the superior characteristics of the Italians of this time. Da Vinci's *Mona Lisa* with her bemusing smile is timeless, Botticelli's *Birth of Venus* is exuberant, and Raphael's *Fornarina* and other various Madonnas are a tribute to women's beauty, seduction, mystery, and fascination that will stand for eternity.

It's no small wonder that we now speak the Tuscan Italian of famous Dante Aleghieri (1265-1321). His *Divine Comedy*, written in the vernacular, is the most important written text of its time. It is a long narrative poem describing a journey towards redemption.

Francesco Petrarca (1304-1374) was the greatest lyric poet of his period, having written over three hundred poems in Italian with patriotic and religious sentiments. Giovanni Boccaccio (1313-1375) wrote the first masterpiece of prose, which is appreciated in a hundred stories known as the *Decameron*. These extraordinary men created a triad of talent, which ignited the imagination and fueled the revival of learning and individualism of the Renaissance.

Leonardo da Vinci (1452-1519) had perhaps the most versatile mind of all and was a true universal genius. His scientific achievements were groundbreaking. Next time you step on an elevator, ride in a helicopter, parachute from a plane, or fly one, think of him. Gyroscopes, mobile ladders, submarines, and the bicycle were all first created in his fertile mind. Any one of these achievements would have been outstanding for a person of his time. When one factors in the *Mona Lisa*, *The Last Super*, *The Virgin on the Rocks*, the first accurate drawings of the human anatomy, and hundred of other inventions, one becomes humbled by the accomplishments of this intellectual superstar.

Today we all take for granted that the sun is the center of our solar system and our earth moves around it. The conventional wisdom of the sixteenth century, including the Church, believed that the earth was the center of the universe and the sun did the revolving. Galileo Galilee (1564-1642) supported the theory that the opposite was true, and he was the first to challenge the all-powerful Vatican, risking excommunication and burning at the stake for committing blasphemy. He, in fact, was put under house arrest for the rest of his life. Pope John Paul II pardoned this heroic astronomer-mathematician five hundred years later for presenting this truth to mankind. Galileo also found time to invent the telescope, pump, compass, and thermometer, among other things. He was another Italian giant that changed the world forever.

"To boldly go where no one has gone before"-- is exclaimed in each episode of the famous TV series *Star Trek*.

The audacious Genovese navigator, Christopher Columbus (1451-1506) did exactly that over six hundred years ago, transforming our society forever by discovering the Americas. He was followed by his countryman, Amerigo Vespucci (1451?-1512), for whom America was named, and by Giovanni Verrizano (1485-1528) and Giovanni Caboto (1451-1498?). All added to the voyages of discovery, opening two huge continents to European expansion and civilization.

The personalities discussed briefly above are of the first category and represent only a small fraction of the greats that Italy produced. Any one of them standing alone would have been the pride of an entire nation. Yet Italy produced hundreds of these individuals. Their efforts enlightened the world then, and continue even today to define our times.

Viva Italia!

A Country Divided

The unification of Italy in 1861 was very much over-due, considering the peninsula's over three thousand years of shared history. England, Spain, France, and Portugal, along with most of Europe (with the exception of the German principalities), had formed nation-states centuries before. They were commanding and in charge of their destinies. Not so with Italy. She remained divided and fragmented, oftentimes fighting fruitless wars internally. The discipline, conformity, obedience, and controlled behavior necessary for union were lacking among the many independent duch-ies, principalities, and republics of Italy. Instead, there often was intrigue, betrayal, scheming, and maneuver. The very qualities that made Italians outstanding in letters and the arts, such as creativity, brilliance, and bravura, were their collective national downfall. When does virtue turn into vice? The Italians, of this period, were over-civilized, com-plicated, decadent, indecisive, and unable to unite under one leader. The population and those in authority did not think collectively, but rather, divisively. Spiritually, they were Italians, but not yet nationally. Not yet! There was no sense of statehood. The citizen identified with his city or town, possibly his region, but not his country. For example, the Sicilians disliked the Spanish Bourbons, as well as the Italian Piedmontese, and with good reason.

The Church, of course, played out her temporal role in this drama. She was always strong enough to keep Italy divided for her own individual gains, but not strong enough to bring Italy together. Oftentimes the popes would make alliances with foreign forces to enter Italy in order to support the Church's needs of the moment. The Papal States, it must be remembered, were large, and hence, had many conflicts and issues with other principalities. The same popes who gave out blessings and dispensations waged wars against their own kind. The total net effect of all this derision was continued failure, delusion, failed expectations, and calamity for all. Yet, things do change for better or worse when bitterness and disappointment reach an unacceptable crescendo.

The Unification

The signs of unification began to appear during the early eighteenth century. Napoleone Bonaparte, a good Italian name if there ever was one, swept away the monarchies and petty principalities. By doing so he inadvertently ignited the republican cause in Italy, which began the revolution for independence called the *Risorgimento*. The shame and humiliation of defeat was self-inflicted, and the populace began to want vindication. They had had enough with the illiterate foreign hoards. There was historic precedence for such sentiment; it was Pope Julius II who commented, *"Fuori i barberi!"* ("Out barbarians!") in the fifteenth century. Poets and writers put pen to paper extolling patriotism, the old virtues of an ancient people. Giuseppe Verdi's music appealed to Italian pride. There was movement and a beginning of collective thinking. Excitement was in the air for all things possible.

The rhetoric and the music fanned the flames of revolution and caused an artistic assault on the foreign enemy. Giuseppe Garibaldi (1807-1882), Giuseppe Mazzini (1805-1872), and Camillo Benso Count Cavour (1810-1861) formed a triad of general, philosopher-politician and statesman that laid the groundwork for the unification of Italy under King Vittorio Emmanuelle II (1820-1878).

We must thank my Sicilian antecedents for the initiation of this unification. During 1860, the islanders were in continuous rebellion against the hated Bourbons. This action invited an invasion by General Garibaldi and his famous thousand Red shirts. There was a Giuseppe Gambino among the brave patriots; maybe he was a very distant cousin of mine. The climatic battle took place in Sicily; near a town named Calatafimi, the birthplace of my patrilineal grandmother. By sheer valor and grit, the outnumbered and poorly armed patriots were victorious. Their battle cry was "Rome or Death!" In 1861, Italy was united under King Vittorio Emmanuelle II.

It was Cavour who announced, "Northern Italy is now made. There are no more Lombards, Piedmonts, or Tuscans…we are all Italians but there are still the Neapolitans." The northern part of the new country made unification an easier task than the south where Naples is located. The north was most European; additionally, it was wealthier, more developed, better schooled, and more able to modernize, hence, a good place to make Italians, rather than the rural Mediterranean south.

Disappointments

Within a remarkably short period of time, the Piedmonts were acting very much like the hated Bourbons of old. High taxes, little development, and poor or no planning were the policies directed at the south.

It was the old system of keeping an anxious populace, confused, ignorant, abused, and poorly governed, with little redress to the law. A few local *grand signori* (the privileged class made up of principally the great land owners) were, however, favored, and did the necessary to keep the people downtrodden. What to do? One could not complain any longer about the rapacious foreign rulers, as they no longer existed.

The policy of the northern Italians towards their southern brethren was one of arrogance and benign neglect. Mixed into this policy was a racist component based on years of ignorance and misinformation. Tolerance towards the south was not to be encouraged, but rather, loathing, which still, to a certain extent, can be observed today in the big cities of northern Italy.

In fact, I never quite understood why, when I went to visit my clients in Milano, they always emphasized my New York City breeding rather than my Sicilian heritage. They could not accept the fact that a Sicilian could be as effective and dynamic as I was, and alluded to my fast New Yorker ways. I would insist that I was "*Siciliano, cento per cento*" (a hundred percent Sicilian) to no avail. They would try to placate me with an all-knowing smile and a change in conversation.

Most of my Italian friends, living as I do in Hawaii, are from northern Italy. The same stereotypical joking around continues, albeit in a much friendlier manner. They call me, at times, *Terrone*, which is a derogatory term used to call those from the south of Italy who reside in the north of

Italy. I wear this as a badge of honor and generally respond to them in perfect Italian by calling them *barbari* (barbarians). We all have a good-natured laugh, as time has healed many wounds. If, however, an Anglo-Saxon American were to dare call me WOP or Dago, derogatory terms, which were employed in the USA against Italians, it would be at his peril. Some wounds have healed, not all.

Alas, here in the USA our story has been of success. It is the story of the southern Italian immigrant who made this strange new land his own. It brings to mind the famous salutation of Julius Caesar as he crossed the river Rubicon: "*Veni, Vidi, Vici!*", ("I came, I saw, I conquered!") Indeed we have!

La Miseria

We are getting ahead of ourselves here, as it is necessary to recall that the nightmare of injustice had returned to haunt the peoples of the south of Italy, known as the Mezzogiorno. During this period, which began shortly after unification, taxes went up over 40 percent for the *contedini* (simple people of the land), while the rich *latifondisti* (great land owners) paid little taxes at all. Loans were taken against the land of the poor *contedini* to pay off these taxes at exorbitant rates, and it was often consequently confiscated. In 1865, 1 percent of the population owned over 50 percent of the land. Local industries that were thriving under the Bourbons went out of business because of measures taken by the new government. *La miseria*, or misery, was rampant. There was little food, little water, much illness, no education, and huge unemployment. I remember my grandfather's friends in conversation mention *pane e cipolla* (bread and onions) to indicate bad times with little to eat.

A new and novel phenomenon became popular among the common people. This was the image of the noble banditry in the Robin Hood mode of stealing from the rich and giving to the poor. It was not quite as exotic as the old Errol Flynn films portrayed it to be. When the Piedmont soldiers arrived to make the Sicilians submit, the young men took to the hills. Hit and run was their strategy, as in days gone by. Often, the men would visit their families, bringing hot food right off the local rich landowner's table. These men organized into groups which in time became the infamous Mafia.

The well-known crime organization does not require comment in these pages, as there are so many other sources available to the interested reader. However, there is subtle usage of the word "mafia" in Sicily, which is defined by a great sense of self-esteem, self-respect, haughtiness, and fearlessness. Luigi Barzini, in his masterpiece titled *The Italians;* mentions that one can hear said that a good-looking and high-spirited horse was mafioso. I have never taken offence when, either in jest or not, I was referred to as mafioso by those who knew me, as I assumed the term was meant as a compliment. In that regard, it had nothing to do with the feared crime organization to which I do not belong.

To illustrate this mafia way of comportment, my grandfather would often entertain me over a good hot bowl of lentil soup with stories of the old country. His father, my great-grandfather on my mother's side, was enterprising, and, therefore, although not rich, owned some small parcels of land. My grandfather went out nights to tend to the sheep, accompanied by three faithful dogs and a trusty *lupara* (a sawed-off shotgun). Grandfather was told to be helpful if any of the "friends" (Mafia) were to pass by unannounced. One fateful night, a group of men on horseback came by his country shack. He was terrified, as these men had a strange aspect, long beards, wild eyes, and they were heavily armed. They ordered grandfather to give them water and food quickly, as they were in a rush. Upon leaving they swore him to secrecy, --*Omerta`* -- not a word. Not many hours after they left, the Piedmont soldiers arrived and questioned grandfather regarding the wanted men who had shortly passed through. It was easy for him not to answer, as he could not understand their Italian. He spoke only the Sicilian dialect. "Vedi nuddu-Sacciu nenti!" (I saw nobody-I know nothing!). He was lucky they did not shoot him on the spot; perhaps his tender age saved him, for he was all of twelve years old.

Months later, the same wanted men passed by the shack again and left all manner of foodstuffs for the entire town. They referred to my grandfather as *onorato* (honored one) for not betraying them to the *stranieri* (foreigners) and for being mafioso. It was good to have friends in those uncertain times.

My eyes were wide open with excitement as he told me the story, for in my mind I was convinced that my grandfather met not an unknown Sicilian bandit that night, but Robin Hood himself. By the time I got to school to tell my friends, the story took on some embellishments of my own making. The first recount held closely to the facts. However, by the time I was telling it the fifth or sixth time, the Robin Hood persona became none other then my very own grandfather. Looking back now, I realize I committed a child's exaggeration, as I was only nine years of age. Then again, upon reflection, perhaps it was my grandfather riding in the night, stealing from the rich to give to the poor. God bless his soul.

*My grandfather Tommaso Sparacino and
his mother, Sicily, circa 1898*

The Diaspora

What earthly reasons could there be for people to leave their known surroundings for the unknown? *Diaspora* in Latin means a scattering-- in this case, the largest European exodus ever. Untold millions of people of the Mezzogiorno were uprooted and thrown to the winds, never to return to their native land again during the sad period of 1861-1926.

O Italy mother of us all!
Your shine shall always be
When I arrive on that dark
foreign shore
I shall not forget thee
--your author

Why leave beautiful Italy? Why trade a pleasant climate for one not as clement? Why go to a place so alien and not hear your mother tongue spoken; that wonderful lyrical sound no more? The food, the customs, and one's own family will have changed forever. The image of fourteen-year-old boys bidding farewell to their mothers in the piazza of their hometowns and promising to return soon, but never to do so, was excruciatingly sad. Much heartbreak was experienced in this enterprise of going to the new world. Was it worth it?

Yet, the only option to survive *la miseria* was to emigrate. The new government of the north spread about the seeds of this Diaspora. They never admitted their blindness or the foul deeds they perpetrated against their own brethren of the south. These *contedini* with little skills, illiterate, poor, and desperate, nevertheless were among the most heroic peoples of this earth. Among them were my dear grandparents who took matters into their own hands, and made a success of their lives in America against all possible odds. *Bravi*!

My Maternal Grandfather

The trip to America took approximately twelve days by ship. Most emigrants traveled in steerage. They were incarcerated below decks, with few facilities and poor food, as they endured seasickness and its known consequences. Children traveling alone and pregnant women suffered the most. My fourteen-year-old maternal grandfather, Tommaso Sparacino (1890-1961), left Sicily for New York on a passenger ship in 1904 at the tender age of fourteen. He was brimming with health, and, therefore, had no problems with being accepted to the new country. Imagine the others who were not so fortunate, who were sent back immediately for medical reasons. It meant another twelve days on the high seas to return home and to *la miseria*.

Once my grandfather passed the gauntlet of Anglo-American officials at Ellis Island, who had the power of acceptance or rejection, he arrived in his new world, New York City. Tommaso was met by a distant cousin and brought to a basement apartment in Ridgewood, Brooklyn. It was a two-room affair shared by four other immigrants.

I remember him telling me about his first meal in America. He was left alone in the apartment on the first day of his arrival, as the other men were off working for a dollar per day. Apparently, there was no food, and my very hungry grandfather was desperate. He searched the apartment and, as luck would have it, he found a piece of old and very stale bread. What a find! He immediately held it under the water faucet, which made the treasure more easily eaten. He gulped it down as if it were a gourmet treat. Welcome to America!

It is no wonder that during the many years I had the good fortune of living with him, I was never allowed to waste any food. He would take me shopping with him in our Italian neighborhood, located in Ridgewood, Brooklyn, every Saturday. That is how I learned to shop with a discerning eye and for only the amount that was required.

First we would go to the chicken market, where we would make a big thing about selecting just the right bird for our table. Lots of discussion would ensue between the proprietor of the market and my savvy grandpa. The price seemed always too high and the quality not up to our standards. Some things never change! Live chickens were held in cages for inspection and once selected for sale, were killed and plucked on the spot. I often remember the smell and sounds of the spectacle when I now shop for my family in our very antiseptic food store for a packaged chicken. Shopping was more fun with Grandpa, and I knew the bird was always fresh, not frozen.

We would dash to a number of other shops, such as the butcher, fish store, and finally, my all-time favorite, the bakery. Palermo and Canepa Bakery was located on Knickerbocker

Avenue right in the center of Brooklyn's Little Italy. The fragrance of the sweets and pastries was extraordinary. There was always a line of people there, so we would take a number, American style. As we waited, my Grandpa would gossip with his acquaintances in Sicilian dialect. I was not much interested in what they had to say, but in later years, my linguistic talents, augmented by the dialect picked up at the bakery shop, would serve me well.

I would urge Grandpa to be sure to buy the canoli, which were sweet, creamed-filled tubes of delight. There also was a large selection of cookies, and, at the end of the counter, there was a lemon ice machine. I always got one for being a good boy during our outings. Life was good with Grandpa.

My grandfather was born in the year 1890 in a provincial town named Giuliana. He was very strong and handsome. He told me once that he was born with a small tail, which was removed surgically at birth. In the countryside of Sicily, that was a sure sign of supernatural strength. He was a cross between Rudolph Valentino and Cary Grant. His hazel eyes betrayed his foreign Norman blood, while his Greco-Roman profile revealed his mixed heritage. He was, as a young boy, a shepherd--a child of nature who survived by his quick wits.

Many were the times, at the tender age of twelve years or so, he and his dogs, Bardacco, Vespa, and Principessa, would have to fight off the hungry wolf packs that roamed his father's lands. The dogs often would get the worst of the fight and he would have to save the moment by firing his handy *Lupara*. Imagine the swirling action in the dark, with the dogs growling and mixing it up with the snarling wolves. As he told me this story, I would imagine the alpha male of the pack charging directly at my grandfather while he held his ground--BAM, BAM!! The shot hits the hungry wolf between the eyes and the wild beast goes down just inches away from his smoking gun. He would order the dogs to take up the fight again, and this time, with the pack leader dead, they would be successful and save the sheep.

Grandpa's personality was already developed when he immigrated. Often upon entering a room people would immediately notice him. Our dogs would tremble by his mere presence, yet I never saw him abuse them. He worked as a coal truck driver for McCollum Coal Company before retiring to take care of me. He started by making a dollar a day, and often worked seven days a week driving a horse-drawn truck through the streets of Brooklyn. Although he was rough and tough, he always treated me with kindness and love. I was the son he never had, being the father of three daughters, one of which was my mother, Gaetana.

He, of course, was the master of the house, as things were his way or no way. Sitting at the table to eat was a ceremony. I would not dare touch a piece of silverware until I got his nod. He rarely had to give the dogs or me any verbal commands, as a knowing look was all that was required. I always felt safe and confident around him, and knew what was expected of me. I remember him telling me that if anyone ever made the mistake of bothering me, then he would fix them good. I feared no one or anything, for my grandfather was always there for me.

Grandfather never needed the advice from many of the "How To Bring Up Children" books and films that are out on the market today. He never had to sit me down to explain things to me. He taught and guided me by example; be strong, be honest and honorable, and never yield was his mantra. I only remember him once telling me to never forget who I was and where our family came from. It is amusing to note that regardless of my grandfather's admonition, it took me most of my adult life to really appreciate that I am a true Sicilian, *cento per cento*, and that I am a descendent of a very old, rich, and noble culture.

The saying that the streets in America are paved with gold was steeped in falsehoods, yet many abroad believed that was the case. Certainly the Rockefellers, Morgans, Vanderbilts, and the like had made huge fortunes in the days of laissez-faire and monopolies. However, that was not the case with the Gambinos and the Sparacinos. My antecedents were faced with bigotry, unfairness, low wages, cruelty, physical abuse, and sometimes death.

The first mob lynching of Italian immigrants in America occurred as early as 1896. The "we" group of local inhabitants and the "they" group of new immigrants created a schism that fueled decades of hatred in America. Perhaps World War II was the turning point in time when assimilation occurred in mass. Better to hate the Hun, and not the WOP. Having a common foe went a long way in bringing people together. The old story repeats itself time and again.

Our American twentieth century, in the end, belonged to Sinatra, DiMaggio, Como, Graziano, Mancini, Lombardo, Lombardi, Andretti, Mosconi, Lanza, Pacino, Valentino, Talese, Coppola, Scorsese, LaGuardia, Iacocca, Scalia, Pelosi, Alito, DeNiro, Alda, Lasorda, Valenti, Giuliani, and many others--too many to mention here. The immigrants and their offspring helped to define this country and the world at large. Their style, grace, and shear eloquence, along with hard work, were their common gifts to the new world. It must be genetic, as this period produced a rebirth, or Renaissance, if you will--one of many that Italians gifted to the world. Imagine if they had not come!

Sicilian Shepherds circa 1900

*My grandfather Tommaso Sparacino on his wedding day
with his bride, my grandmother, Rosaria. New York, 1911*

Our Way

"One works in Milan, one eats in Rome, one sings in Naples, and one gives orders in Palermo"--Unknown.

Although a great generalization, this saying helps us appreciate the many differences there are among a so-called "united" people.

Let us take Palermo, which is the regional capital of Sicily, as an example. There is a comfortable decay and decadence about the city that alludes to its past grandeur. The inhabitants' history is a result of three thousand years of colonization by the Phoenicians, Romans, Arabs, Normans, French, Spanish, etc. This rich complexity of cultures, over time, has given the world a well-defined and a particular type of personality that the continental Italians do not fully understand to this day.

Sicilians are known for their ability to control situations. They do this by being cunning, quick, and clever. The art is to break down any given situation into its simplest part and then provide solutions in bits and pieces. Never be in a rush, and above all, show little emotion. If controlling events means avoiding the law and ignoring rules of the game, so be it.

The idea is always to be ahead of the *fesso* (fool), who is challenging you at the moment. The goal is to win and be looked upon as a person of character and maturity, with great depth and consistency. This type is called *uomo di rispetto*, or a man of respect. One must be respected by one's own peers in order to be considered manly. Fair play, sportsmanship, and the like are looked upon as mere stupidities, weaknesses, and a complete waste of time. It is considered better to be skillful, subtle, mysterious and disingenuous.

The Italian Family

Imagine the impact on the newly arrived immigrant of the American alien shore. He became more mysterious and introverted. He was cut off from the norms and customs that were his guides to life. Hence, the family, always a center of Italian life, now became more entrenched as an institution.

The family was made up of blood relationships, each holding a niche within the structure. The father was, of course, the patriarch and his rule and word were supreme. He was the boss, *il numero uno*! He cultivated a sense of control and seriousness, which displayed his sense of maturity. A true man of few words, his masculine approach to things was underlined by patience, pride, aloofness, and self-denial. His major role was to provide a firm, but just rule over the members of his immediate family. To some degree, this also held true with regard to his nieces, nephews, and others who came to seek out his wise council and kitchen table wisdom.

To be a real man, you first had to protect your family and guarantee its survival. One must always be alert to dangers and use cunning and deception if necessary to disarm any threat. By doing so, you play out the role and your function that is needed by all those concerned. One should never be considered a *buonaccio*, or a good-guy, as it is better to be considered clever, able, distant, and fearsome.

A scene from the exciting film *Pirates of the Caribbean* features Captain Jack Sparrow having a drink with his first mate. Captain Jack and the sailor toasted each other by saying, "Take what you can; give nothing back!" I was struck by the simplicity and pureness of the thought. It rang true; the good captain was not a *fesso* (fool), but a *furbo* (clever one). I recognized the meaning of the Machiavellian philosophy immediately, as my elders had planted it in the far recesses of my mind a long time ago. To survive at all costs and do what you must to protect your loved ones are virtues handed down to us by this greatly admired Italian philosopher of the fifteenth century.

Life outside the family confines was merciless, cruel, and dangerous. The American Catholic Church, in the first decades of the last century, was controlled and staffed by the Irish. Likewise, the governmental authorities were in the hands of the American *stranier (foreigners)*. They all were to be avoided unless you knew someone who could make contacts for you. Keep your distance from the powerful unless you knew them as one of us. Friendliness was a show of fear and uncertainty. It always seemed better to ignore the locals, as they generally knew nothing of our way.

My Mother

Mothers are the soul of the Italian family. *"Mamma mia!"* is perhaps the most commonly used exclamation in Italy. All ages and genders use it generally when facing one of life's challenges, either trivial or life-altering. It often is the last thing dying Italians would utter as death closes in. It is our mothers to whom we turn for solace, warmth, and sympathy. No wonder women nurture the Italian family--they are the glue that unites the parts together, making them run in unison. If the father is king, then the mother is the power behind the throne. The great facilitating role of the Italian mother is more difficult to perform than the father's. She must never appear to be controlling or competing with the father, but merely advising and always supportive.

The kitchen was my mother's realm, where no one would dare interfere in the cooking unless invited to participate. The shopping, cooking, and serving of the food to our family took on an aspect all of its own--a *rason d'etre,* as our French cousins would say, or a "reason for being."

My seamstress mom worked six days a week and could only perform the culinary ceremonies on Sundays. I would awake to the clang of pots and wonderful smells of garlic sautéing in the early morning. Her only day off was dedicated to the evening meal. She would call us to the table with pride, and made sure we ate hearty portions of a well-balanced dinner. It was her way of guaranteeing herself that we could face the next week well nourished.

On occasion, I would be allowed to invite a friend over, and naturally, the family protocol dictated we feed him. On the odd occasion, an Irish friend would sit at the table, and I would be astounded to see his eyes bulge out at the bounty set before him. Poor thing, all he would have to eat was dreary boiled potatoes when he returned home. Gastronomically, it was more fun and tastier being Italian. Mom's delicious tomato sauce recipe follows:

Mom's Tomato Sauce

What you need:

1 onion chopped finely

3 garlic cloves chopped finely

3 tbsp extra virgin olive oil

1 pound of tomatoes

1 small can of tomato paste

2 tbsp sugar

1/3 cup red wine

1/2 cup fresh basil chopped

14 ounces of spaghetti

2/3 cup grated parmesan cheese

How to cook:

Place the tomatoes in a pot and boil until the skin begins to peel. Drain and peel off the remaining skin and discard. Dice the pulp and hold off to the side.

Heat the oil over a low flame in a frying pan and throw in the garlic and onions. Sauté approximately two minutes or until they start to soften.

Put the diced tomatoes into the pan along with the garlic and onions, and continue to sauté for a few minutes.

Combine the tomato paste, basil, wine, and sugar, along with the garlic, onions, and chopped tomatoes in a pot. Bring to a slow boil, adding salt and pepper to taste.

Lower the flame and simmer for five minutes while always stirring the contents.

Spoon off the extra oil if some should collect at the side of the pot.

Cook the spaghetti in another pot by bringing salted water to a boil. Read the directions on the box for al dente results, generally ten-twelve minutes are needed.

Drain the spaghetti, then put it in a large bowl, and add the sauce, and cheese.

Servings – 4

Buon Appetito from Gaetana....

*Right to left Dad and Mom with sister Anna
as brides-maid at their wedding,
New York, 1936*

The Gambino Family,
Grandfather Vincenzo & Grandmother Antonina are third & forth from the left, New York, 1938

The New World

My mom and dad divorced soon after my birth (1941). I lived with my grandfather and adoring mother in a cold water flat in Brooklyn, New York (my grandmother Rosaria passed away before I was born). There was nothing special about us, as the majority of families lived as we did. I thought, in those days, aside from the odd Jew or Irishman, the whole world was made up of Roman Catholic Italian-Americans like us. Over 80 percent of the student body of my school was either second or third-generation Italian-American. Even the faculty had many of them holding teaching positions that were generally held by Jews and Anglos in my mom's day.

Mom's time, the early twentieth century, was severe on immigrant children. She, to her last days, would recount a tale in which she explained that her first grade teacher, Mrs. Schiffer, changed her perfectly beautiful Italian name from Gaetana to the less attractive Teutonic version, Gertrude. Poor thing, she hated it. To tease her, I would call her "Gert," which never failed to get things moving.

One must marvel at Brooklyn's capacity to welcome so many people of diverse backgrounds. It was called the melting pot, where all people mixed to seek the American dream.

That was the theory, at any rate. Each part of the borough, be it Flatbush, Bensonhurst, Ridgewood, or Canasie, etc., had its own personality, while sharing things in common. Perhaps that was the ingredient that made for a successful community at large. We, as kids, would play stickball and jump rope in the streets, which we shared with the cars and trucks. On the ever-present stoops sat the adults, keeping a discerning eye on the children while they gossiped away. It was not organized, but rather spontaneous. To be sure, the adults administered discipline when needed. Many a slap was received by a wayward kid, and oftentimes by a non-blood relative. The street vendors were always present with all sorts of goodies for us kids. A nickel got you a hot knish (snack food consisting of a filling of mashed potatoes) or a cool lemon ice. The place was alive with all kinds of action and sounds.

Brooklyn's weather was intense, cold and wet in winter, as well as, hot and humid in summer. Oftentimes, the firemen would turn on a Johnnie pump to cool off the kids with a strong spray of refreshing water during the torrid summer months. Those who were older would seek refuge from the intolerable heat by going to McCarran Park Pool. It was always crowded, with standing room only, and it smelled badly of overdoses of chlorine.

The long hot summers were punctuated by famous block parties, which took place often. The elders would have the police barricade the streets to vehicular traffic. There was always the ubiquitous beer keg in the middle of the street and all kinds of food made by the denizens. The adults would dance to music in the streets, often played on their accordions and guitars. The children would run around, adding to the atmosphere of mirth and good cheer.

Children became grownups easily in America. All one had to do was get a job and pay one's own way. Many people would harbor the thought that you were as good as your last paycheck. One had to be connected! So at the ripe old age of twelve, I got my first job at Roma Food Market delivering groceries. It paid only one dollar per hour, but the tips were very generous. It was hard work, and it seemed that everyone living in tenement houses were on the third floor and bought the heaviest groceries. I pushed my wooden wagon with big steel wheels noisily up and down innumerable streets, in all sorts of weather. Perhaps that is how I honed my driving skills when, later in life, I drove my Alfa Romeo Spider sport car on twisting Italian roads with great dexterity and speed.

Oftentimes I would be delivering groceries in my own neighborhood, and would see my friends by their frosted windows in their homes, all cozy and warm with Mommy, while I was outside, working hard in the dreaded cold. I felt a sense of accomplishment and superiority to know I was helping to pay my own way. I bought my mom an ironing board with my first pay. Yes, I was often cold and tired, but I was no baby; I was a man!

The Italian Persona

Unwritten rules and norms, handed down to me by my family, governed my actions and lead me to my roots. It is these roots which are inherited from native Italians, who, when confronted with the American scene, dictate Italian-American demeanor. It is this inheritance that ensures a human and refreshing exuberance, regardless of the sometimes hostile local environment. Italians are lively, restless, and notoriously undisciplined, while totally enjoyable at the same time. They do well unsupervised, with little direction, structure, or guidelines. They are master improvisers. Their chaos is strangely controlled. In their disorder, there seems to be an unexplainable order. Plan B is their mantra. From this matrix, the Italian-American personality evolved.

In Italy, the pursuit of happiness, then, is the first order of business. How else can one explain the six-week vacation or the three-hour lunch? The most surprising thing is that many non-Italians want and do imitate this model. The carefree feeling permeating the environment, and the wonderful food, clement climate, fashion and beautiful people everywhere you look in Italy leads to an overall sense of well-being approaching euphoria. One cannot imagine living life in one of those organized, regimented gray countries of the north, where everything works, but where life lacks the joy of making it all worthwhile. The Italians always knew that when dealing with ephemeral time, it was better to savor each moment to the maximum. This is the ethos the Italian-Americans spring from and use to confront the realism of life in the USA, although not always successfully.

Who Are We?

Our Split Personality

Richard Gambino (not of my family) author of *Blood of My Blood*, an excellent work on Italian-Americans, discusses at length the dilemma of the Italian-American split personality. One half of our personality was developed within the confines of our families; he calls it the *Via Vecchia*. It is reflective of traditional and historical inherited norms. The other half is a creature of the contemporary experiences or the Anglo- American way. The former is infused with cleverness, agility and cunning in interpersonal situations, while the latter identifies by a sense of fair play, universal amicability, and the following of Anglo-American mandated rules of behavior. There is an eternal conflict between the two personalities that many first and second-generation Italian-Americans struggle with throughout their lives. Which is the authentic self?

A graphic example is illustrated in a challenge I had received, while I was twelve years old and living in Brooklyn, to fight a big Irish kid over an exchange of family insults. He approached me in traditional boxing form, with fists raised in the ready. I dispatched him quickly with a swift kick to the groin. He had no chance. I won, but I did not feel vindicated for having defended the honor of my family. I felt rather guilty for not playing by the rules. To this very day, I cannot predict what I would do under similar conditions. It is truly vexing.

Uncle Bill

Another graphic example of this confused sense of being is well illustrated by a favorite uncle of mine through marriage, William Mario Capodici. Uncle Bill, who, by the way, physically resembled former King Faysal ibn Al-Aziz of Saudi Arabia, often reminded me that he was proud to have been conceived in Marsala, Sicily, and born in New York City. Bill's father was a doctor from an educated Sicilian family, who had to emigrate because of political reasons, as he supported the anti-monarchist movement. Thus his family was not the typical unschooled and unsophisticated emigrant prototype. Perhaps this explains Bill's distinct anti-social attitude towards the ignorant immigrant masses, the crude Anglos, and the newly arrived middle class. He was an accomplished barrister and served the City of New York as corporate council for many years. He defended the city against what we now call "police brutality" cases. He once confided in me that many policemen were "bums with badges." The inference was to not assume that officialdom will do the right thing, and rather, to rely on one's own devices. How Sicilian, yet he defended them, how American! The dilemma continues to appear in many forms and often. My mom, for instance, would often shudder when Bill would ask her to dance at one of the Italian-American weddings we attended frequently in those days. Oh, they danced well

enough, but Bill had a peculiar habit of commenting nega-
tively on the other couples dancing on the floor in a loud
voice using the Sicilian dialect. "Gert, look at that *pezza de
bottana* (whore)", or "*e chissu e` culo* (and this is an ass)", etc.,
etc., ad nauseam. My mom would die of embarrassment, but
nevertheless would mimic him at home in front of me until I
would burst out laughing. Having known most of the targets
of his invectives, I must admit he was more right than wrong
in his appraisal of the cast of characters involved, particularly
with regard to their physical attributes. Billy Boy was so
proud to visit me in Rome, and also a trifle bewildered by
the Italian scene. The fourteenth-century palazzo, the ever-
present elegant Romans, the clothes, and the food were a bit
overwhelming for him, as he was, in the end, and in a strange
and contorted way, part of the Italian-American dilemma.

As time passes, I find myself agreeing with him and his
awkward points of view as I, too, have little sympathy for the
crude, overindulged and over fed newly arrived SUV crowd.
In memory of Uncle Bill and his wife, Aunt Ronnie, I have
taken to wearing his graduation ring, which I inherited. In
this way, I feel closer to them, now that they have passed
from the scene.

Bill's children, my cousins, with whom I played and
lived across the street from, were very different in their life
approaches than I. As they were of second-generational parents, they were more tuned into the contemporary American
scene. They were of the *now* people and knew very little of
the Italian way, the traditional way. In contrast, my first-gen-
erational upbringing gave me a reactionary view of things,
more old school, if you will. Although we loved each other,
went to the same schools, and spoke the same language,

we inhabited different worlds. They lived by the Anglo-American rules, while I either ignored them or invented my own *all'italiana*.

Finding Ourselves

Oddly enough, many Anglo-Americans admire and copy many of our family customs and ways. They have embraced the ethos and culture of the endless television programs, films, and written works of the Mafia families. The sagas of the Soprano and Corleone families and numerous others have replaced the old westerns we watched as kids. Michael Corleone, the Godfather's son in the film titled *The Godfather*, is the new hero, and has replaced Roy Rogers in the public's eye. Imagine, the Mafia has replaced Cowboys and Indians! Perhaps the lack of depth, passion, and loyalty in today's typical American contemporary scene has created a void that can be filled only by celluloid fantasy.

A possible explanation for this phenomenon is the unprecedented economic freedom we experience in America as a displacing force of the family unit. Relatives, who once lived across the street from each other generations ago, now live, at times, three thousand miles away. My closet blood relatives live six thousand miles away from me. The good life in the USA requires little structure and protection. The result of this exuberance can develop into a feeling of uneasiness, emptiness, and sense of loss. Apparently, a little adversity is a good thing, as it tends to bind people together, which is the foundation of the family. People needing people, and not institutional or governmental solutions, are what make for a happy, well-rounded life.

This ongoing process of change is discussed in Kenneth Ciongoli's and Jay Parini's book, *Passage to Liberty*. They make a convincing argument that Rome was reincarnated in the USA by Italian immigrants. They illustrate that the Italian transplanted culture has developed in the fertile soul of the American dream. There is much to be said for the extraordinary efforts of the immigrants and their contribution to the greatness of the USA. One can be proud of these accomplishments and more. In many ways, we are one with our immediate environment, and this is a direction one could take. Perhaps, in the end, we will have been so enveloped by our surroundings that we will no longer recognize who we were or are. Is that important? Yes it is!

To be sure, there is an ongoing dilemma and loss of identity for the Italian-Americans. For us, there is little left of our culture that we are familiar with. Yes, we eat Americanized Italian food; we may be able to mumble a few Italian phrases; we may vaguely know of some of the great Italian personalities of history, and that Don Corleone was one of them. The entire issue of who we are as a people has been discounted. We are a percentage of the original, as we are living in America, not Italy. It is said, in the halls of academia, that the most constant thing concerning humankind is change. But what kind of change is possible and desirable for happiness to be the constant?

I believe our happiness is to be found, in great measure, in the percentage of our heritage that we can retain, or, better yet, augment, resulting in the reduction of this discounting of ourselves as a people and of our culture at large. *Esse Quam Videri*, which is a Latin phrase meaning "to be, rather than to seem," was the course I followed in my personal quest of our collective being as a people. Over many years, I was able to reduce the cultural discounting of my Italian personality, and, in so doing, I discovered who I really was and wanted to be in the future.

The hard part, I found, was deducing there was a dilemma at all. The aimlessness, or rather my aimlessness, took on a life of its own. We are all searching for answers sometime in our lives. Why not look systematically at where it all began? Italy, after all, is the scene of our beginnings, as noted previously in past chapters of this book. In order to make a profound and valuable search, one must speak the language of the land. That is what separates the dilettante from the serious and passionate researcher.

My Personal Return

Studying and speaking the mother tongue made me feel inclusive. A whole new world opened up to me. I began feeling Italian, and as if I had just returned from a very long trip to be with my own people again. Indeed I had.

Things began to shape up rather nicely while studying at the University of Perugia in Italy during 1962. After those first few difficult weeks of speechlessness, I actually could speak in Dante's tongue rudimentarily. After three months, I took my first examination in front of three stern-looking Italian professors, and I received a decent 28 over 30 grade. This is equivalent to a B+, which is not bad for a person who could never understand English grammar, much less Italian.

With my newly found language in hand, I decided to visit Sicily, the land of my origins. As can be imagined, I was excited to finally see the place of my grandparents, and to do it not as a tourist, but as a card-carrying Italian student. It made a world of difference to be able to communicate with the locals in their tongue.

There was a dream that visited me often after my grandfather's demise, which played itself out in real life. In the dream, I would find myself at the bottom of a hillside, looking up at a medieval town of the fourteenth-century period named Giuliana. One day while I was in Sicily, I found myself at the bottom of a hillside, at the foot of Giuliana, which was eerily similar to the one in my dream. I started walking up the hillside and arrived in the main piazza. I was breathing heavily, as the sun was hot on my face, but the cool breeze that caressed my body urged me on. There to my left, as in the dream, was a café. I did not want to go on, but my feet were moving me along involuntarily. All at once, I burst through the hanging beads, which shaded the entrance, startling the noonday customers who had come for a drink. Unlike in the dream, however, my grandfather was not there waiting for me…but more importantly, I was. It has been many years, and I never had that particular dream again. I had returned home. To this day, I believe my grandfather spoke to me from above, via that dream, lovingly guiding me, as he always had in the past.

Left to right: Aunt Ronnie, Uncle Bill and
Mom at a reception New York 1965

Closing The Circle

My Big Chance

The Jews were scattered by the Romans from Judea over two thousand years ago, causing their diaspora. In 1948, they returned and reclaimed their identity in what was their land. By contrast, it took me thirty-five years to reclaim mine. Although I did not have the all-powerful Roman Empire to contend with, I did have toxic assimilation, ignorance, and indifference to confront on a daily basis.

It is somewhat straining not to be part of a whole. After all, most of my Italian-American friends and family were getting on with their lives where they were born. When, in later years, I saw a list of former classmates, I was astonished to find that over 70 percent of them had settled within thirty miles of our high school in New York. 70 percent! One pays a price in order to live life contrary to the established norms; however, with some good luck, the rewards can be swift, outstanding, and unexpected.

I was rewarded as I found myself walking smartly down Fifth Avenue on a crisp Manhattan morning in October of 1969. There, on the corner of Fifty-third Street and Fifth Avenue, I spotted an amazing thing. Right in the storefront window stood a recreation of an ancient Roman scene, with columns and busts of Caesar. I wandered in before I realized I was in the ticket office of Alitalia Airlines, the flag carrier of Italy. I was elated to hear correct Italian spoken again, and I commenced to make a facetious reservation in order to keep the illusion that I was going to Italy for as long as possible. Between the usual questions and answers necessary between agent and client, I managed to ask, in Italian, if Alitalia was offering employment. Within ten minutes of my question, I was sitting in the personnel department, filling out an employment form. I gladly accepted a position as a reservation agent, unfortunately cutting the salary I was then making by over 50 percent. No more selling high priced cosmetics to affluent retail outlets for me! Now it was selling Alitalia by phone to my own people, and many times in Italian. I would have paid for this privilege! Beyond the sheer pleasure of working for the Italians, I also was given the privilege of free airline travel. Imagine, weekends in Rome, or anywhere, for that matter. I quickly racked up the miles, flying to all of the cities I had always dreamed of. Venice, Florence, Palermo, Buenos Aires, and Rio de Janeiro were mine for the asking. I could hardly believe my good fortune. I had Italy on demand, along with the rest of the world, and I was paid to enjoy it.

As sales was my forte, I moved rapidly within the organization, and in a few short years I was working in the marketing department at the New York head office of Alitalia, which interfaced with Rome daily. It was there that I would hear about a position with United Airlines in Italy, as described in a previous chapter. This would be the next step in closing the circle. Thus, Alitalia was my passage back to where I wanted to be, allowing me to retake my true identity, and live and work among my own people. I will always be grateful to Alitalia, which facilitated my journey to retrace and capture my origins. I was about to end my diaspora by working and living in my beloved Roma.

The Joy of Living in Italy

Italians love a show, and being part of it is entertaining for them. Hence, my arrival in Italy in 1975 was met with great fanfare. There were moments of absolute joy as I began my seven-year posting to Rome. The luxurious Excelsior Hotel was venue to my introduction as United Airline's Director for Italy. Approximately 150 *cognoscenti* were in attendance to welcome me and cheer me on. It was like a Fellini film, as everyone was dressed in the latest fashion. My Hicky Freeman suit could barely compete with the Zegnas and Armanis worn by the guests. I gave a modest speech of thanks, and was astonished by the hearty applause that I received. I felt a bit giddy as I realized that these people wanted me to be successful. As the evening wound down, a Mr. Fabrizzio Serena, the number two of Alitalia introduced himself and his lovely wife, Giovanna to me. I had met Fabrizzio briefly five years earlier when I was in Washington, D.C. Fabrizzio, although modest, was a baron and was married to a countess. In addition to his aristocratic bloodlines, he had a terrific personality, with depth and great polish. He became my mentor, and we did many wonderful things together at work and at play. One of my fondest memories of him is when I would take him out to lunch, picking him up in my vintage Alfa Romeo Spider. He would always ask to drive the car, and then proceed to wheel through the Roman traffic with great *élan*, while regaling me with the latest airline gossip. Fabrizzio raced Formula One Ferraris! Indeed, those were heady days for a kid from Ridgewood, Brooklyn. The *dolce vita* was real, and fate allowed me to play a role in it that I shall never forget.

Of course, it was not all fun and games. Life had its ups and downs, and the high corporate standards of United Airlines kept my nose to the grindstone. In a strange turn of events, I, now as United's man in Italy, had to represent the country at various and sundry meetings all over the world. My opinion was often asked regarding the Italian situation at the highest executive levels at United Corporate. I was now the voice of Italy. The dream was worth the gamble; I was clearly living beyond the thirty-mile limit of my school chums.

The American executive was admired throughout the world in the mid-1970s. Italy always had a love affair with the USA and, hence, my boss always enjoyed coming to Rome for a visit. Of course, there was a press conference and written comments given by me to the trade to commemorate the latest visit. We often used the Gold Room of the Excelsior Hotel. The furnishings were exquisite, as was the eighteenth-century Baroque architecture. As I stood before a mixed group of travel professionals, surrounded by oil paintings and gold leaf, I felt taken by the moment; thus, I ignored my dry, prepared speech and made extemporaneous comments to those seated before me. Hence, I inserted a different dialogue to explain our current midyear results, comparing them to my competition in other European counties. My comments given in Italian went like this:

"Italians listen to me; today is a historic day, a day of decision! Italy once again is at a crossroad with regard to our latest revenue figures. We say "NO" to the competition in Europe! I report to you that Italy has vanquished Spain; we have conquered Great Britain; and we have completely defeated Germany!"

The crowd went wild and started cheering me as if we were at a soccer match. I heard my name repeated in cadence for the first time in my life:

"G-a-m-b-i-n-o-G-a-m-b-i-n-o-G-a-m-b-i-n-o!"

"*Numero Uno, Numero Uno, Numero Uno!*"

I roared back over the din, "Today Italy, tomorrow the world; long live Italy!" Pandemonium erupted as the no-longer-seated guests came to hug and kiss me at the podium, men and women alike. My boss was spellbound, having never witnessed such a performance before. How prophetic, United Airlines would become a world carrier within a few years.

With regard to my supposedly off-the-cuff remarks, I knowingly used, in part, a famous speech given by none other than the fascist leader, Benito Mussolini. I must have read it somewhere and used his syntax and body motions as my own. The crowd loved it and so did I.

My Ancestors

The Gambino and Sparacino Families

My paternal grandfather, Vincenzo Gambino, was born in Torretta, Sicily, in 1867, and my grandmother Antonina Marchese was born in Calatifimi, Sicily, in 1866. They were married in 1889. They were adventurous for their times, as they did not get married in a traditional Italian marriage ceremony, but eloped. Antonina came from an old and rich Sicilian family, which owned vast lands, while grandfather Vincenzo came from a family of professionals. The Gambinos were pharmacists dating back from the Bourbon era. Antonina was duly disowned by her family, cast out of her comfortable surroundings, and banished for the man she loved.

Vincenzo, a tailor, worked in some of the big-name shops of Palermo. As the economy worsened, he, too, had to look abroad for work to support his growing family, and also to escape the wrath of the Marchese of Calatifimi who never forgave him for eloping with grandmother. His first attempt at immigration was in the immediate neighborhood. He went to Tunis, Tunisia, in 1894, a mere 125 miles from the coast of Sicily. From there, having worked for the

French colonials, he left for Marseilles, France. Unlike most unskilled emigrants, he had a trade, which was sought after and, therefore, presented him with choices. His last attempt at emigration brought him to the very gates of America, to New York City, in 1898.

He never returned again to his homeland, but, rather, sent for his family. Here, his last child Adolfo was born, who would become my father. The Sparacinos, my Mom's family, were another story altogether. I have already written about grandfather Tommaso, the sheepherder and adventurer. He, too, emigrated to America at about the same time, approximately 1904, later married Rosaria Giarrocco, and had three beautiful daughters, one of which, Gaetana, became the wife of Adolfo and produced a male child in 1941--your author. The lineage of *Jures Sanguinis* is therefore irrefutable and complete. I am Italian by blood, as well as spirit.

As I mentioned before, my parents divorced shortly after my birth. That is how I came to live my formative years with my mom and my maternal grandfather. The Sparacinos were a beautiful, vain, and proud people, with a rather myopic view of life, as the vast majority had at the time. I met the Gambinos when I was twenty-one. I began to understand why I was not as good-looking as my mom's family, as the Gambinos were of very common and average appearance. But the wit and intelligence of the Gambinos were leagues and scores above anything I had ever seen before, and rarely after. I adored my father at first glance. He had wit, charm, and a great sense of humor. He inspired me to the limits of my abilities. After meeting him, I quit my mundane job as a hairstylist and went off to college. I had a lot of catching up to do.

My dad graduated from New York University cum laude, and did it at night, while working a fulltime day job. I graduated from Bluefield State College cum laude, and did it without having to work. It was not the big-time university my dad attended, but, in a sense, I reached a level allowing me to approach his achievement at a more leisurely pace, albeit with a lower academic content and challenge. Be that as it may, I enjoyed sending him my grades at the end of each semester. I wanted to please him, and make up for all those lost years. I know seeing those A's had a pleasant effect on him. After all, I did it to try to walk in his footsteps. In the process, I learned about the world and the possibilities it could hold for me. Dad lived to see me transfer to Italy, and, in fact, he predicted it years before it happened. He was so proud when I would speak to him in my Tuscan Italian. Those were great visits together, talking for hours without a stop, playing chess, and recounting to him my many adventures abroad. Although he has passed on, the word "dad" still tugs at my heart. I use it often with my father-in-law, as it is a natural thing for me now to do.

I had lots of uncles on the Gambino side of the family. My uncle Tony, a barber by trade, sticks out most in my abbreviated memory of my dad's family. My mom and I were on a bus in Queens, New York, one day, and, as fate would have it, we were both standing and hanging on to straps as the bus negotiated the infamous potholes of the city. As the bus stopped for a traffic light, my mom brought my attention to a barbershop not forty feet away from us. In the shop stood a distinguished barber applying his trade. My mom exclaimed, "That is your Uncle Tony; I always liked him!" As my hair needed a trim, a few days later, I strolled into my uncle's shop. I remember sitting in his chair and having the usual mundane discussion one has with a barber. "Not too short on the top and a little off the sides." Uncle Tony did not have a clue who I was, and commenced cutting away. The law in New York directs all barbers and hairdressers to display their licenses with picture by their particular work-station. I had him! I waited until he finished my cut and then I started my line of questioning while looking up at his license. "So you are a Gambino, eh!" The answer came swiftly: "So what is it to you?" Now we must remember that this was the same Uncle Tony who did three years in prison for gunning down an Anglo who persisted in calling him a WOP many years before. I knew I was on shaky ground. So I immediately followed up with "That is a lovely name; in fact it is my name, too, and Adolfo, your brother, is my father!" He warmly embraced me. He immediately closed his shop, and off to lunch we went, to catch up on twenty-four years of story. Of course, he informed me that he was the only one of six children who was born in Palermo, the city, while the other children were either born in the countryside or in America. My pranks on him would continue for years. On my last visit to him before his death, I addressed him in Italian, as he had not known of my studies at Perugia; he could not comprehend my linguistic abilities. That did not stop us from having a great afternoon together, drinking black coffee, and eating canoli. Uncle Tony was a pistol and he knew how to use one, too.

After meeting my Gambino relatives, I felt more complete, and could answer more confidently those many questions from people wanting to know if I was related to the famous Carlo Gambino, the alleged godfather of the so-called

Mafia in America. My standard answer was "not the same family, but certainly the same tribe." Of course, it does not help having the first name Thomas, for Carlo's oldest son is named Thomas. We are approximately the same age, and we both have that certain Sicilian look about us. Carlo arrived in the USA in 1921 illegally aboard the SS Vincenzo Florio. He was met by his cousin's family, the Castellanos, and began his alleged life in the Mafia. He was a small and very slight man with a hooked nose, who always spoke softly. Despite his fame and fortune, he lived modestly and operated very quietly. He was both adored and feared. His influence lasted over 40 years and his family was the strongest in the nation. He was often compared to a Machiavellian prince, conjuring up all sorts of clever action and dispensing with his enemies quickly and without fuss. It was believed he used his considerable power and influence to keep drugs off the streets of New York City. Certainly, the police were not as successful and, therefore, Carlo's charmed life continued. The Sicilian rule he applied was to ingratiate oneself with those in power, to do them favors, so one day one could call them in. Sound familiar? He achieved a Renaissance of power and influence during his time. Many of those he dealt with, either private citizen or political personage, miss his omnipotent presence, and so do I.

Obtaining My Italian Citizenship

Article 1 of Law N. 91/1992 confers recognition of Italian citizenship on those people born abroad who meet certain criteria. The law is based on the principles of *Jures Sanguinis*. Essentially, the Italian government recognizes citizenship based on blood. As I mentioned previously, I have the hundred percent Italian variety from both sets of grandparents. If one were to make a comparison using wine as the standard, then it is like having Corvo di Duca di Salaparuta, an excitingly spicy and elegant wine produced near my grandparents' ancestral lands, running in one's veins. *Cento per cento*, one hundred percent, the *Vitis Vinifera*--the wine grape species is not mixed, but is kept pure, giving the product its thundering taste and great longevity. No wonder the invading Greeks called our land *Oenotria*, the land of wine, centuries before the birth of Christ.

After 130 years of migration, the Italian governmental authorities have reached out to Italians born abroad. By recognizing this birthright, we can reverse, to a certain extent, the tragedy of the terrible Diaspora that befell us those many years ago. The essential issue here is truth of being. I am different from our co-citizens in America. I have nothing in common with the German-, British-, French-, Spanish-, or African-Americans, other than having a history of conquering, colonizing, and civilizing what is now, after the fall of the Empire, their ancestral lands. Surely, these very different peoples have a sense of their own collective history, to one degree or another, as they should. I ask only to be recognized as an Italian; nothing else will do. It is who I am, what I want, and what I have to be, now and forever.

Bureaucracy, according to *Webster's Dictionary*, is "(1) a body of non-elected government officials, (2) an administrative policy making group, (3) government characterized by specialization of function, adherence to fixed rules, and a hierarchy of authority and (4) a system of administration marked by official, red tape, and proliferation". The definitions are extraordinarily precise, and I salute the many lexicographers who, through a collaborative effort, so knowingly described what we as citizens are up against when dealing with the government. No doubt one can understand that it has taken well over two years to gather the documents and the various collective official statements from various and sundry bureaucrats to arrive at a proof of citizenship. In the process, I made many acquaintances that were truly helpful in my quest for recognition. Jan Noto, a dear Italian-American friend, tops this list of notables. She single-handedly, while touring Sicily, got the relevant documents relating to my ancestry. With little knowledge of Italian, but with great determination, she prevailed where others less committed would have certainly failed. But, in retrospect, that was the easy part, as on the USA side things were even more challenging and tangled. It was only through other intermediaries in the USA that I was able to be successful. We shall touch upon that in a later chapter.

Economics-all'italiana

All Is Not Well

It is painful writing about the less attractive side of things in Italy. In presenting one's views, one should always try to remain honest and balanced. It is then with a sense of melancholy that we now look at some of the shortcomings of Italy today.

The country continues to be a pleasurable experience for most people, as it has been over the millennia. To be in Italy seems so normal as it is a kind of natural oasis for the human spirit. We need not dwell on her many charms here as we have encountered them in previous chapters of this book. Suffice it to say that life in Italy is *dolce* and replete with the joys of living.

Yet, the current bigger picture is somewhat skewed and has changed over the past years, as Italy's economic competence has declined and stagnated. One may sense a malaise among the denizens, which is hard to visualize or define. If you were to inquire too directly of the locals, the entire apparition could disappear in a puff of smoke, perhaps camouflaged by an excellent meal.

We, however, must take off our rose-colored glasses and not be dissuaded by the ever-present sumptuous environment. This is the difficult part, for Italy is in many ways magical. She can manifest herself to the astute observer in many variations and themes. We will bravely endeavor to carry on and try to shed light on the current issues, not as academics, but as genuinely concerned individuals interested in the root of these contemporary problems. We shall also attempt some likely solutions to the on going difficulties.

"It's the economy, stupid," is a very effective political battle cry. The phrase, likewise, highlights what is all so wrong in contemporary Italy. As reported in *The Economist*, in the November 26, 2005, issue, the Gross National Product (GNP) of Italy is 80 percent of Great Britain's, whom Italy eclipsed in the 1980s. The near future, as well, looks dim and unattractive. Italy is in a downward spiral resulting in lost market share, especially in its largest export markets, France and Germany. Its traditional export product base, which has always been textiles, shoes, and heavy manufactured goods, are being under-priced by more cost-effective producers, particularly the Chinese.

The European Union, of which Italy is a charter member, is part of the global economy. Hence, it is no surprise that this body has opened its markets to the Asians among others. As an aside, it was General De Gaul who predicted back in the 1960s that the 21st century would belong to China. This was a master stroke of prediction back in his time. They work harder for less to produce many products which Italy specializes in. The old game of devaluing the lira to undercut the competition is no longer an Italian option. There is no lira; Italy's unit of account is the euro, which is tied to other EU members. Grandiose deficit spending, the country's way out of economic stagnation, also is forbidden by the EU rules. Those rules, which apply to all members, legislates limiting deficit spending to a certain percentage of the GNP. There is no longer the government cookie jar to go to for assistance.

What to do? Obviously, it is not business as usual, but rather, what is needed, in my opinion, is a draconian attempt at a redesign of the broken Italian economic model.

Globalization, liberalization, privatization, and, above all, transparency are the basic ingredients that need to be put in motion with a sense of urgency, in order to move forward and encourage investment. Further, research and development must be increased many times over to fire up the Italian innovative spirit, resulting in competitive products and prices. Essentially, Italy cannot or should not try to out-Chinese the Chinese. She must go to another level, which involves putting to use her native genius and entrepreneurial spirit to restore her rightful market share.

Suppose, for a moment, that our thesis, as put forth, is correct. Who then will enact such bold but necessary policies? The many past governments have wasted years in power doing little to overcome the economic decline. Odd, as Mr. Berlusconi, the former prime minister is the richest man in Italy, worth reputedly five billion dollars, which he made on his own. What happened? Nothing! In his defense we must understand that it takes more than one man, no matter how much economic acumen he may possess. His government was made up of six divisive parties, each vying for their own agenda. The old divide-and-conquer rule gives just enough influence to control the strings of power for power's sake, but never enough to make a real difference for the country's sake. It all sounds very familiar. The fatal Italian characteristics, which kept Italy divided and weak for many centuries before unification, continue to be in play here. The sober coming together for the greater good of society is lacking, causing poor and disappointing results on the world's economic stage. The center-left wing government of Mr. Gentiloni also has many divergent agendas. Apparently, there is a consistency in being ineffective on both sides of the political spectrum.

Some of the more fashionable diagnoses are that Italy is like the ocean liner *Queen Mary*, trying to sink in three feet of water. Another one heard, from time to time, is that Italy is above the mundane economic rules and need not follow them as other lesser states must. NONSENSE! Italy is rapidly turning into a side show and a relic of her extraordinary past. It has happened before. Just reflect for a moment on the decline and fall of the Roman Empire.

Absolutely no one can denigrate the last seventy-some years of Italian democratic rule, brought to us by approximately the same number of governments, which followed the fall of Fascism. A peaceful extension of the franchise was directed to the masses by the ruling elites. Real democracy was achieved after twenty years of brutal dictatorial rule under Benito Mussolini. However, we have seen that the economic changes needed are not achievable under the present fractured and devisive political leadership.

Drastic times require drastic action. Hence, the solution requires that an expert nonpartisan team of the best minds in academia and the commercial world should be organized by the Parliament to make the changes to the economy, based on modern current precepts as partly discussed above. Let us call these experts the "Team for Renewal," and award them the power necessary on a five-year basis to bring about the much needed reforms, with minimal interference from the divisive political side. By so doing, Italy will have the possibilities of a rebirth, and will be able to reclaim her role as leader and teacher to a very needy and waiting world.

Rebirth

My Special Son Nicola

In Torretta, Sicily, my paternal grandfather's place of birth stands an imposing monument in the main piazza. It is dedicated to the fallen heroes of WWI. On one side are inscribed names of the Gambino men, many of whom were connected to our family by blood.

In 1996, I had the happy occasion to show my then five-year-old son, Nichola, the monument. I wondered if he could understand the significance of the structure as he looked up at it, locking it in a strong gaze. As it turned out, I need not have been concerned as he said to me, "Daddy when I am a big boy, I will come here to see again. I was struck; my son more than understood…I knew then that he, too, was a true Gambino. I was so proud and happy to have this son; is there any wonder why I love him so dearly?

In retrospect, one can understand why a man would give up the many female companions in his life for that special one. The variety, while stimulating and enjoyable, leaves nothing to compare with the product of a beautiful monogamous union. A son like Nicola is so special. He is in many ways more of a Gambino than I am. The wit and sharp intelligence reminds me of my own father. This, along with great musical talent and sportsmanship abilities, would be enough to make any father proud. But no, there is much more. Nicola is a very handsome lad with dark penetrating eyes set in a face of alabaster. He reminds me of a cross between a young Marlon Brando and Jean Paul Belmondo. It is difficult to not show him off. Thank goodness he has no ego problems with me around. We enjoy so many experiences together; for a second year in a row we spent six weeks in Florence, Italy, studying the Italian language and culture at the Societa' Dante Alighieri. He also had the opportunity to do sculling training on the Arno River with the sons of the *cognoscenti* of the city. I was extremely proud to see him solo rowing out under the Ponte Vecchio with the tourists looking on. It was a brilliant way to develop his own Italian persona. Italian is now his second language. All of this was accomplished at age fourteen.

During the winter months, Nicola attended a prestigious school in Hawaii called Kamehameha Schools, named after the great king who unified the islands in 1810. He competed for one of the limited spaces available and was among the first picked as he was in the upper five percent on the entrance examination scores. The school is a great institution and one of a kind, which was set up by Princess Pauahi in 1887 to educate her people. Hence, one of the qualifying criteria to enter the school is to have some Hawaiian blood. Fortunately, Nicola meets this requirement, because my beautiful wife is part Hawaiian. So it is like having two sons, one Italian and one Hawaiian. I am blessed and love both parts of this special child, and thank my wife for giving me this joy.

In 2010, Nicola was accepted at John Cabot University to pursue a four-year undergraduate degree in International Affairs and Communications. Thus began the next phase in his personal journey. JCU is an American liberal arts institution situated in the heart of Rome's Trastevere. There was no need for the usual doubts and fears surrounding studying so far from home. Nicola embraced his new Roman residence with a strong determination. JCU was more than the usual reading, writing and arithmetic. It allowed Nicola to absorb his new culture first hand in the country of his lost inheritance.

It was with enormous pride that we attended his graduation ceremony at the lavish Villa Aurelia in 2014. The stunning views of eternal Rome along with the sumptuous surroundings underlined the fact that our son had found his true persona in the country of his forefathers. He is my hero in doing the right thing in finding his way. In 2017 Nicola, after working a year in Rome, has returned to Hawaii. He is now an MBA candidate as he continues to grow and embrace his duel culture.

In boca al lupo! (good luck)

My Lovely Wife Catherine

Catherine Leila Kamaka was born in Honolulu to Sam and Gerry. Sam, a Hawaiian, and Gerry, who is French-Irish, had the most beautiful daughter. Katy looks like Eva Gardner and is all the things I am not. She is patient, meticulous, kind, soft, and very understanding. I met her in an elevator in London. She was dressed in a hula outfit, which had the scent of fresh cut flowers. I literally breathed her in--how I wished that we would get stuck between floors. I fell madly in love with her within seconds, going from the third floor to the fifth. I knew I had met the special one, as the many others paled in comparison. We met again three weeks later in Lugano, Switzerland, as she was part of a hula team that came to assist me in a promotion for United Airlines in nearby Milano. Walking, under an umbrella while it softly rained at lakeside, was magic. Her beauty was in sync with the outstanding surroundings. The pureness of her being intoxicated me; I simply could not go on without her. I should have kidnapped her on the spot, for it took me five long years and much effort to win her to my side. The last 30 years of our lives together is a kaleidoscope of happiness. Her love saved me from the depraved and morally corrupt life I was leading. Our life together has brought out the best in me. I shall love her ad infinitum.

Italian Citizenship

I became as an Italian citizen on September 2, 2005. That day I received a telephone call from the consul general's office, informing me that my Italian citizenship had been recognized. My friend and former colleague Romana Bracco along with Roberto Falaschi, Consul General for San Francisco were instrumental in over-coming the bureaucratic maze, Their action allowed me to acquire my recognition as an Italian citizen at long last. Needless to say, this sent me into raptures of joy. I was a shooting star for the entire day. As I was home alone cooking, I played my favorite Italian music, Ricardo Cocciante, Andrea Bocelli, and a few Sinatra CDs…"Fly me to the moon and let me play among the stars." I sang my heart out in my non-singer voice. Yes, this was big, and an achievement of a lifetime! It can happen and one can change fate. By arriving at this plateau I felt I had struck a blow for all the Italian immigrants and their offspring against the painful Diaspora that had occurred so long ago.

While I was living in Rome, a journalist acquaintance, Marco Ambrosini, once dedicated a book to me, as follows:

"Thomas, you are the most Italian of all the Americans."

Today, however, he could write that I have become "the most American of all the Italians." Things have changed forever!

How timely it is that this book's first printing should have coincided with the glorious ending of the 2006 Winter Olympics in Torino. In Pragelato, Italian Olympic history was made by Giorgio Di Centa, with the gold metal win for Italy in the cross country ski race ending the games. His dramatic sprint through the final stretch was typical of the bravura and great style of an entire nation. Moments later, parachutists trailing streaks of red, white, and green smoke honored the Italian win as they descended down from the azure sky. The entire nation was jubilant, as were my son and I, watching the triumphant scene on TV these many miles away. Later in the year Nicola and I were in Rome as Italy won The World Cup soccer match. We participated in the Roman explosion of joy and sang out, "ITALIA! ITALIA! ITALIA!". The party went on for days.

These occasions helped to highlight my conviction that it is better to have been Italian at least part of one's life than never to have been Italian at all.

Closing Advice

In a sense, the pages of this book are like a series of love letters--love letters to my fellow scattered Italians, to my friends, to my family, and, most of all, to my dear wife and son. In these letters I have tried to summarize our historic migration, along with my journey of self discovery. I have tried to pass on what I have learned so that it might promote well being and understanding in others. My final words are for those who might benefit, but especially for my son Nicola.

"Never give up" has been my mantra; get as much exposure as possible, as early as possible. Stay out of the box; be contrary to the ordinary, the common, and the mundane. A sign that you are thinking beyond the usual mode of your contemporaries is that you are often in disagreement with them. This is a good sign! Simply put, Mom, Military, and Marriage, while safe and comfortable, are limited. Strike out, make mistakes, and when you fall, get up and start over again. Those who do not make mistakes in life are not living to the fullest. Make a difference and fear nothing.

Find something you feel passionate about; look for a cause and make it your own. Create achievable goals and find the way to arrive at them successfully. Even if you do not fully arrive, you will have traveled, and that, in and of itself, is fulfilling and creates a happy condition. You can measure your progress by how well you accommodate life's opportunities. "Carpe diem!" Seize the day and enjoy life! Along the way, give back to others and help make a difference in their lives, by example and by using your force of ideas. Make a praiseworthy matter, superior, and take a superior matter to the maximum.

Always be good to yourself, as that is your very first responsibility.

My lovely wife Catherine, 1981

Your author with family, Torretta, 1996

Let's Q&A

Keeping with a just and balanced approach of many points of view, I invite you to sit in on some Q&A exchanges I had with my Italian friends. It is my pleasure, therefore, to introduce Mr. Umberto Mucci, an Italian living in Rome. He is an accomplished writer, CEO and founder of 'We The Italians" an informative Italian/American web site.

Umberto, how do you account for the inspiring achievements of Italy in history, culture, art, music, literature, science, discovery, statesmanship, cuisine, ETC?

-The enrichment of waves of diverse cultures over the millennia to Italy, in my opinion contributed vastly to the extraordinary accomplishments the country bequeathed to the world. Add to this the clement climate, the totally beautiful environment and the innate intelligence of the natives and you get a full picture.

Why, not withstanding Italy's dazzling world-impact, has its national history been so mediocre?

-We are a new country, younger than the USA and yet we possess thousands of years of shared history as part of our DNA. A major flaw that we share is an extreme sense of individualism, local pride and a lack of coming together for the benefit of the many.

Can you describe the Italian national character and way of life?

-We are a people who have seen it all and invented most of it. As we have had experienced periods of suffering we tend to befriend our fellows when in need. As and example, take into account the extraordinary efforts put forth by the Italian Navy in saving so many lives of immigrants on the high seas, more then half-a-million alone have arrived over a three year period. This from a country the size of the State of Arizona!

We are humane and display it on the world stage at large. A vice could be our individualism brought to an extreme while a virtue would be our collective ability to overcome the challenges to everyday life in an artful way.

Can you describe the Dolce Vita?

-Dolce Vita expresses the Italian joy of living. The interfacing of beautiful people, the food, brilliant light that is everywhere, the lyrical language, style and a sense that life is magical and only can be enjoyed here. For sure it has evolved from the early Felinesco period to the more updated version of today. Life has become much more complex and fast paced. The Dolce Vita lives!

Has former P.M. Renzi made a difference?

-I am not a true Renziano but I do give the Italian PM credit for trying to turn around the country by creating a more successful model of governance. The goal, although somewhat elusive, is to simplify the tremendous bureaucracy for more transparency. Individualism again is at play here with few power holders wanting to sacrifice for the many. The old dilemma tends to repeat itself.

What is Italy's economic profile?

-There is very high unemployment, approximately 40% among the young and 15% for the more mature population. The reasons are many; one of the most glaring is the answer given above. Also, as in many modern states, corruption is widespread and debilitating. The EU, to which Italy belongs, has also a sluggish economic profile although recently improved. The amount of Italian R and D is pitifully low when compared with other modern states.

What temporal role does the Vatican play in Italy today?

-Essentially, The Vatican plays a less temporal role in government than in the past. It does exercise however a moral standard that is still felt in the halls of power not only in Italy but also around the entire world. It appears that Rome still commands respect and clout globally. 1.3 billion people look to Rome for guidance. In a sense the Roman Empire has not fallen but merely morphed.

What is the Italian mood regarding the EU?

-Italy needs the EU and vice versa. While frustrated by yet another layer of bureaucracy in Brussels, the reality is that the time of the nation state has passed favoring union with others. There will be no Italexit and many are not sure that Brexit itself will survive. Only time will tell!

Tell me something of the current immigration crisis?

-The current wave of immigration from Africa and the Middle East is critical for us as we are located in the middle of the Mediterranean, the major escape route for tens of thousands of disparate people fleeing for their lives. It's a pity that Italy's ability to fast start their lives is limited when many of our European partners seem not to want to share in the burden. Yet we continue to endeavor to save lives on the high seas everyday. It is a global problem not easily solved by one country alone.

Will Italy continue to share its way of life with the world?

-Italy as always will embrace its life style and share it with the world. We will survive the harshest test and as believed by many, Italy will be the last to turn off the lights on the human experiment.

Our next Q&A is with another Roman friend who prefers to remain anonymous. I can share that he is an executive and very current with all things "Italiano".

My friend, how do you account for the inspiring achievements of Italy in history, culture, art, music, science, medicine, cuisine, discovery, ETC?

It is not easy to respond to this question with only a few words; as I believe that a series of causes are interlinked. Naturally the central role of Roma Caput Mundi (world capital) in ancient history has contributed to inspire the world's development of culture. Ancient Rome was a true center of attraction for those who desired to grow culturally. The Romans had a percentage of reading and writing equal to today, almost 100%. Most schools were free. But even after the fall of imperial Rome, in Italy the Vatican maintained alive the interest in culture although targeted to their goals. In fact, it is in the Italian Churches that we find the most significant works of art of the Medieval and Renaissance period along side libraries and written history of events.

Also in music, the sacred choruses contributed to develop somewhat daring experiments and new musical instruments while many other cultures had only drums to make music.

Maybe the history of Italy filled with domination of many different peoples brought Italy to be culturally everlasting, with respect to other countries. Let us remember the quotation of the great Italian writer, painter and politician Massimo d'Azeglio; "We have made Italy, now we must make the Italians". In fact the State, often absent from the needs of the citizens contributed to initiating the idea that the Italians have to do all things themselves. Also the lack of caring for the needs of the people in some periods of Italian history contributed to the waves of Italian emigration to other countries. They, nevertheless, maintained the very identities which contributed to the development of Italian culture worldwide. With regard to the inspiration of cuisine that Italy has shared with the world, it is based a great deal on the high quality of products the country produces. This has permitted Italian cuisine, in part, to become famous worldwide.

Not withstanding the enormous impact that Italy has had on the world why has its national life been so mediocre?

I believe that the responsibility for Italian mediocrity in its national life falls on the politicians. However, the politicians have been voted in by the Italian people and, therefore, it is their responsibility. Most Italians think only of their personal interests and not that of others.

Can you describe the Italian national character and their way of life? What are their virtues and vices?

As it happens in most countries the virtues of the Italians change depending on if one is born in the North, Central or South. In the north the state is more present, the people often have good jobs, do not have many problems facing them in life because there is the necessary infrastructure. Often the climate is severe. This condition generally makes people more serious regarding work but less cordial and inward. In the South to the contrary the State is always absent. There is little work and the infrastructure is missing likewise. However, to compensate one lives in a marvelous place in a Mediterranean climate. This clement weather generally make the people more cordial and friendly and it gives one the feeling of doing what is necessary to live ones life day to day but always moving ahead. Perhaps here is born the exact spirit of the creative Italian way of life.

In the center particularly Rome the neighborhood with the "room of power" it makes people want to interfere a bit as they all have a friend who can recommend a quick acceptance to a hospital, find a good seat at a concerto, and to find a job. These friends are often considered people of influence and can pull strings. Often times they are less educated then the majority of the populace.

Speaking in general the Italians like to eat well, do not like to work too much, they are in general not disciplined, are very attentive of how they dress (bella figura) and Italian men consider woman pry to be conquered.

Can you explain La Dolce Vita? Does it still exist?

La Dolce Vita is a symbol used to define a historic period that took place in Italy in the 1960s. In that period of the economic boom the Italians thanks to the Lira exchange rate could finally buy the Fiat 500 and a washing machine. That was the period when the world viewed Italy as the center of beauty and fun. In reality La Dolce Vita was simply a commercial idea to sponsor our country. Now the debts that remain are strangling our economic system. In fact, Italy is the country where one pays more direct and indirect tax.

This does not mean that in Italy La Dolce Vita is finished but to live it there is a minimum of Italians.

What is the economic profile of Italy? Why so much unemployment? Why are people disgusted with the government?

Today the public Italian debt is 2.200 billion Euros. Any economist would say that Italy is a failed state. In fact, it is still on its feet only because the will of strong powers that in this moment do not have interest in Italy becoming like a failed Greece or Spain. The only state of the European Union that has gained of the common currency has been Germany. It has doubled its exports while the other states have remained stopped or like Italy which has a weak recovery. Naturally, an economy that does not function, the products that do not sell, with little money in circulation to control the debt can only lead to unemployment. Everybody has understood except the European organisms or perhaps they have understood very well but that was their objective…the people are disgusted in general, but if one were to analyze the history of our country the people have voted for 40 years for the Christian Democrats and the Italian Socialists and then 20 years for Berlusconi. The left has not done better in these years. Just think that the Prodi government brought us to Europe destroying the Italian Lira for an iniquitous exchange rate. This fact has redoubled all of the costs for food and of housing as well. The beauty is that we had PM Renzi and presently PM Gentilone who were appointed to office without a vote of the people. As I explained before it has been the major part of the Italians thinking of their own personal interests who have voted in people that did not favor the national interests. To add, the majority in our country is subservient to power and give constantly distorted information to please their bosses.

Has PM Renzi made a difference? Is he valid?

Renzi is a valid person above all if we had to promote a set of pans or mattresses. The pity is that all this commercial capacity of sales of Renzi has been put at the service of the big commercial powers of Confindustria (trade organization of large firms) and not at the service of the Italian people. Renzi has made the national situation worse, for example he had taken away article 18 of the Constitution that prevented owners, bosses to fire people from their jobs with out cause. Hence, today a new employee cannot get a mortgage to buy a house or a loan for a car. Renzi has left in tact all of the bureaucracy that derives from the provinces which he has promised to simplify. He lost a referendum to simplify the governmental structure and therefore resigned. We now have PM Gentiloni and more of the same.

Does the Vatican have an impact on Italy in general?

Actually governmental parties tend to have support implicit or not from the Vatican. The politicians give their assent to the Vatican in order not to have problems with the Church. In Italy, hence, the Church has a great impact politically and socially. Besides the goal of the Church has always been that of domination of the population and I do not see why it should change now in contemporary times.

What do Italians think of Brexit...will there be an Italexit?

Italians are beginning to understand that the European Union does not favor them. In fact, with the gigantic Italian public debt to many entities and foreign banks, Italy has few possibilities to leave the EU without failing. In that case, it would experience many consequences such as a depreciation of the new unit of account (Lira), vanished estates patrimony and poverty diffused to try to imagine a sustainable future.

Brexit is not important to the Italians, on the other hand the UK has maintained the Sterling per the European Union Constitution. Italians in general are not interested too much in the affairs of other countries, as long as it does not affect the interests of Italy, or if the media harasses them.

What is the impact of emigration from Africa and the Middle East on Italy? What is the solution?

Italy is subject to very heavy immigration flows. Our country in the first 10 months of 2016 has received over 300,000 people. Fortunately for Italy many of them pass on to other countries with a more stable economy. The problem is that these countries are already saturated and the moment will arrive in which they will block emigration from Italy. Italy cannot block the emigration from Africa and the Middle East because it is engaged on badly conditioned boats often without control. The only solution to avoid this emigration is to help these poor countries to create a sustainable economy. In substance, there is no need to give a fish to someone starving but rather a fishing rod and teach him how to fish.

Will Italy continue to embrace its life style and share it with others. Will it continue to teach the world?

It pleases me to think that Italy will always be a beacon of culture for the world even though it is not a stable country. I believe that the way Italians live will not change. Certainly, it is reasonable to think that in the next 50 years there will exist in Italy a large Islamic community acquired by the Italy that will have different values then those currently; sort of like what happened with the Chinese community.

I think that thousands of cultures are difficult to be forgotten.

Our third Italian friend is Dr. Michele Carbone, born and educated in Italy and is the Director of Thoracic Oncology at the University of Hawaii Cancer Center. That is Michele's day job as he is a true Renaissance man with multiple activities. EG: I love his risotto....

Michele, how do you account for the inspiring achievements of Italy in history, culture, art, music, literature, science, medicine, discovery, statesmanship, cuisine, ETC?

Two reasons, one is genetic, the other is the long bi-millennial culture we have.

Why not withstanding Italy's dazzling world impact has its national history been so mediocre?

Italians think that they (each one of them) knows better than anybody, so they do not follow orders, they change orders, resulting in chaos, and it is very difficult to make them work as a team. You see that in everything. For example, where do we excel? The arts and sports where we play or compete alone: painters, singers and musicians, cyclying, archery, tiro, etc. The fact is that a team will always outperform an individual, Any mediocre soccer team of 11 would beat Maradona or Messi if they played alone. So Italy does well in some things and bad in others.

Why did you relocate to the USA, EG: professional or other? Where did you first live and when?

Because of curiosity, I was offered a position at the National Institutes of Health (NIH), which supposedly had some of the best scientists in the world. I was curious to see if I could measure up with them. I worked at the NIH in Bethesda for 8 years then moved to Chicago and then to Honolulu.

What were some of the challengers you had to face? EG: professional, integration, language, culture? What were some of the more easy things for you?

The environment at the NIH was very welcoming and stimulating, there were about 100 other Italian "fellows" learning how to compete at the top level of medical research, I had a wonderful time. We worked 7 days per week, from 8 am to about 900 pm, I had a 3 year old daughter Martina and a wife who was a scientist like me. We alternated to pick her up from day care at 500 pm, bring her to the lab and she learned to hide under the bench when security came around because it was forbidden to have kids in the lab. So probably bringing up a child that young when both parents work so much was the main challenge I faced. I brought the issue to the NIH director, I said look you guys say you support families, yet here we are with a daughter who spends her evenings in a lab full of radioactive reagents and infectious viruses, who has to hide under my desk, when NIH security comes around–kids were not allowed in the labs, so we can do our work. We need a day care and an after school program here on campus. The great thing of this country is that if those in charge think that you have a good idea, they listen to you even if you are a young foreign person. I was a fellow from Italy, yet the NIH within a few months formed a committee to build a day care, and a couple of years later they built a nice day care/after school program on the NIH campus to meet the needs that I and other parents faced. My daughter never had the opportunity to enjoy the day care, as we moved.

What are some of the things you like or dislike about the USA?

I like that if you have an idea and you want to do it, even if initially someone inevitably will try to discourage or stop you, if you insist, and if you believe in what you want to do, you can do it. I do not like American coffee, I still drink only espresso.

What do you think of the Americans in general as opposed to the Italians? What are some vices, virtues of their way of life?

America is a big country, with many different cultures. For example to what should I compare Italy to the environment in Washington DC, Chicago or Hawaii? Each one of them is totally different, and north and south of Italy are different too. In general, Italians have a longer history, so they are more cynical, their hopes were crushed too many times. They have much less hope that you can make any effective changes of the status quo. Americans still believe that it is possible, see the election of Trump for example. But, as someone who has fought to try to change and improve the status quo all my life—and sometimes I even succeeded-let me say that nothing is more difficult than changing it!

Maybe the main difference between Italy and USA is that in Italy it is impossible to change the status quo, and here in the US, it is only extremely difficult!

What do you miss from Italy. EG: the cuisine, the culture, the people, family, la dolce vita?

My mom, of course! And all the friends I grew up with. Having time to ride horses. The pastor coming around each morning with his herd of sheep and with a fresh ricotta, and overall the more relaxed life style and the beautiful Mediterranean sea, the most beautiful Sea in the world.

Do you feel still as an Italian or as an expat? Explain!

I have two passports and I am proud of both.

Would you return to live in Italy if possible? Where?

Of course, one day I hope so. In my house in Calabria on the Ionic Sea.

Do you follow the American politics trends or Italian? Both?

Both, and it helps me understand what is going on in both countries much better. You will see that the same news have a very different spin when reported in Italy or US. For example, I had insisted from day one, as all my friends can tell you, that Trump was going to win, largely because having followed the trends in Europe of people revolting against the political system and the politicians, I expected the same trend in the US.

Tell us something of this great adventure you are on in the USA.

Right now I am focusing on finding ways to prevent mesothelioma, the cancer caused by asbestos, and to identify novel therapies. We made significant progress, I lead the top research team in the world in mesothelioma. I built an international network that includes some of the best scientists in different disciplines and we work together in spite of the geographical distances. It is a terrific team, I will take credit for having assembled this terrific team, and I enjoy working with each one of them. Each year I fly over 160,000 miles to coordinate this research. We just made some very important discoveries, in our own laboratory at the University of Hawaii, and we will announce these findings soon, as soon as our papers are published. So I am very excited about my work and I will keep working until I enjoy doing it. If you want to know more about my work, check out my website: http://www.oakparkpathology.com/

Our final Q&A session is with my friend Zach Dilonno, an Italian-American attorney practicing in Hawaii. He is the very active director of the Friends of Italy Society of Hawaii.

Zach, why a friends of Italy and what is its mission or purpose?

The Friends of Italy Society of Hawaii is a non-profit organization established in 1990 in the State of Hawaii. The mission of the organization is to foster friendship among the residents of Hawaii with an Italian background or with a special interest or feeling for things Italian by promoting a better understanding of Italian culture and traditions of the past and present. The organization aims to provide its own events and programs toward fulfilling this mission as well as provide support to other events.

Does FOISOH interface with national organizations such as OSIA, NIAF?

We were in contact with NIAF who gave us great support in our Festa Italiana event that took place on 07 October 2017. We had an extraordinary success with many thousands of people who came to enjoy our outstanding and exciting Italian gathering. We put Italy on the map in Hawaii and look forward to doing the same in 2018 and beyond.

What are some recurring activities that you have during a given year?

The most popular is our Christmas party that is a sellout every year. Taking advantage of our clement weather we do a beach side picnic that is popular with families with children. A new initiative is monthly diner parties held at one of our sponsoring Italian restaurants. We also do cooking classes, Italian language classes and Italian film events.

How many members do you have and what are their ethnic backgrounds?

We currently have 140 members of a mix of Italians, Italian-Americans and lovers of things Italian. All are welcome and appreciated.

How many board members do you have and what is their function?

We have 9 members currently serving as President, Vice President, Director, Treasurer, Editor, Membership, Secretary, ETC.

What are some challengers you face?

Some challengers are sponsorships, membership registration and internal support.

What are the annual membership fees?

$65.00-family membership, $45.00-individual membership, $30.00-senior and student membership.

What impact does contemporary Italy have on the membership?

Current events plays a role especially news of unfortunate occurrences such as the earth quakes in Central Italy.

Future plans of FOISOH?

-As mentioned we had planned a Festa Italiana to connect with our membership and disengaged Italian Americans along with the general public at large.

-We hope to revive a sister city program between Honolulu and an appropriate city in Italy.

-We are working on becoming a community partner with the Honolulu Museum of Arts.

Give some personal comments please on being a contemporary Italian-American.

I have recently reengaged with my Italian heritage as a result of a recent trip to Italy. Meeting my Italian family members shocked me out of my normal passive existence. Additionally, I was able to extract out of a text on emigration (The Scattered Italians) information that lead to my reengagement and interest in who I really am as an Italian–American.

Epilogue

Our story has covered the movement of an entire people from an agriculturally based Euro-Latin society to an industrially based North American Anglo-Saxon one. We have touched upon the history of the Italians, from its very beginnings through to the present period.

The WHY, WHEN, WHERE TO and HOW they emigrated are no longer secrets to us. WHAT they found and were confronted with, along with my own family experiences, were also part of our dialogue.

None of this drama could have taken place if America had not opened its doors to "the poor, huddled, downtrodden and oppressed masses yearning to be free." It is through her enormous largess that we are able to have a story to tell. There is simply no other nation that has done so much, for so many and for so long.

In my case, America acted as the great facilitator, allowing me to thrive and realize my true identity, while Italy provided me the opportunity to live my dream.

I shall always be the proud son of both lands. It is my sincere desire that my modest writing effort has resulted in shedding light and insight on issues of interest regarding things Italian. Grazie…your author-Q.D.B.V.

Chronology

Circa 2000 BC	Indo-Europeans immigrate to Italy via the Alps
754	Founding of Rome
509	The Roman republic is created
202	Scipio defeats Hannibal at Zama
52	Caesar conquers the Gauls at Alesia
44	Caesar is assassinated in Rome
27	Caesar Augustus is proclaimed the first Roman emperor
476 AD	Fall of the Western Roman Empire
476-982	The Dark Ages with continued barbarian invasions of Italy
1300-1700	The Renaissance period
1796	Napoleone Bonaparte invades Italy
1860	General Giuseppe Garibaldi conquers Sicily and southern Italy

1861	Kingdom of Italy is proclaimed by King Vittorio Emmanuelle II
1870	Diaspora begins with immigration in large numbers to the USA
1898-1904	The Gambino and Sparacino families immigrate to the USA
1925	Benito Mussolini is appointed Prime Minister of Italy
1929	Lateran Treaty is signed by Pope Pius XI and Benito Mussolini
1940	Italy enters into WW II
1945	Italy is liberated by the Allies; Benito Mussolini is executed
1946	A democratic republic replaces the monarchy
1948	Economic boom; Italy becomes a major industrial power
1957	Treaty of Rome creates the European Common Market
1962	Your author arrives in Italy ending Diaspora
2013	Operation Mar Nostrum Italian Navy begins to recover immigrants from the sea.

Glossary

Roman Adages:

Dulce et Decorum est propatria mori!
It is sweet and glorious to die for one's country.
--Horace

Bella matribus detestata!
War is hated by mothers.
--Horace

Audaces Fortuna Juvat!
Fortune favors the bold.
--Virgil

Jacta Alea Esto!
The spear is thrown.
--Gaius Julius Caesar

Si vis pacem para bellum!
If you want peace prepare for war.
--Unknown

Omnia vincet amor!
Love conquers all.
--Virgil

Mens sana in corpore sanu!
A sound mind in a sound body.
--Juvenal

Nil novi sub soli!
Nothing new under the sun.
--Unknown

In vino veritas!
In wine there is truth.
--Unknown

De mortuis nil nisi Bonum!
Say nothing but good about the dead.
--Unknown

Panem et Circenses!
Bread and Games.
--Juvenal

Sic transit Gloria mundi!
Thus passes the glory of the world.
--The Papacy

Sample words derived from Latin:

AQUA - water
Aquatic
Aquarium
Aqua form

FIDIS - trust
Confide
Diffidence
Perfidy

BENE - well
Benefit
Benevolent
Benefactor

GRATUS - thankful
Grateful
Gratify
Gratis

FINIS - to end
Confine
Define
Finite

LEX - law
Legal
Alliance
Legislature

MANDO - I command
Command
Countermand
Demand

MANUS - a hand
Manacles
Manipulate
Emancipate

MORS - death
Immortal
Mortal
Mortification

OPERA - work
Cooperate
Operate
Operator

OS - bone
Ossify
Osseous
Ossification

PES - a foot
Pedal
Pedestal
Biped

PRIMUS - first
Primary
Prime
Primitive

PIRATE - pirate
Piratical

LINGUA - language
Linguistic

PULCHRA - beauty
Pulchritude

PERICULOSA - risk
Perilous
Peril

FAMA - fame
Fame
Infamous

SANCTUS - holy
Sanctify
Sanctuary
Sanctimonious

SCHOLA - school
Scholastic

SUB - under
Subterranean

MAGNA - great
Magnificent
Magnitude

MULTA - many
Multitude
Multiple

MODUS - mode
Manner

www.ingramcontent.com/pod-product-compliance
Lightning Source LLC
Chambersburg PA
CBHW020258290526
45784CB00003B/1289